EDUCATIONAL RESEARCH
A GUIDE TO THE PROCESS
NORMAN E. WALLEN
San Francisco State University

W9-CTF-675

EXPERIMENTAL EDITION

Wadsworth Publishing Company, Inc.
Belmont, California

Designer: Robert Gross

Production Editor: Susan Yessne

ISBN 0-534-00346-X

L. C. Cat. Card No. 73-94232

Printed in the United States of America

2 3 4 5 6 7 8 9 10—78 77 76 75 74

Dedication

As a graduate student, I once attended a party at which a young woman I was trying to impress discovered education was my field. Her reaction was "how dull."

This book is dedicated to all the men and women and boys and girls who have demonstrated how wrong she was.

Wadsworth Series in Curriculum and Instruction

Series Editor: Jack R. Fraenkel, San Francisco State University

Published Volumes: EDUCATIONAL RESEARCH: A GUIDE TO THE PROCESS,
Norman E. Wallen,
San Francisco State University

Foreword

This is an unusual book. Professor Wallen has prepared a
text to be used in introductory courses in educational research
that differs considerably from the traditional. In the first
place, it is one of the first truly inductive texts that I have
seen. Rather than drawing conclusions for students, Wallen provides them with a series of exercises that allows them to experience what doing research actually means. Thus, among other
things, students identify researchable issues, formulate and
analyze research questions and hypotheses, prepare operational
definitions, do library and field investigations, analyze instruments for validity and reliability, analyze the adequacy of
samples and the validity of conclusions drawn from such samples,
analyze data they collect from a sample themselves, and draw
warranted conclusions from these data. The emphasis throughout
is on actively engaging the student in the kinds of operations
that researchers perform rather than making him merely a passive
recipient of information that the textbook provides. As a result, students gain a much greater appreciation of what the
process of research actually involves.

Wallen also provides illustrations of how his students have
handled recurring problems of research design. These examples
not only give students a benchmark against which to gauge their
own efforts; they also help them to realize that research does
not necessarily belong only to experts. It is a process in
which any who are interested can engage and one of which all of
us can be aware. A further unique feature of the book is the
"Author's Comments" provided throughout in which Wallen analyzes
and evaluates previous studies and descriptions presented in the
text.

One personal note. I have used drafts of the text in my
own classes in educational research, and found many students—
initially quite apprehensive and worried over a subject they
considered rather forbidding—liking both subject and text far
more than they had imagined. Many remarked that the text helped
them understand what being an educational researcher might actually mean, and that they were now rather intrigued by the pros-
pect of further (and in some cases lifelong) work in the field.

Jack R. Fraenkel
Series Editor

Preface

To the Reader:

The style of this book differs from the usual text. The reason for this is the author's attempt to devise a format that will make an introduction to educational research the interesting and personally involving experience that it can be, rather than the boring, pedantic ordeal that is so often described by students. To this end several features of the book should be mentioned:

- The use, for the most part, of a conversational tone, rather than a more customary detached, formal writing style.
- The attempt to keep the expository part of the book as simple and clear as possible, without being guilty of oversimplification.
- The use of a particular study throughout as an on-going vehicle for providing examples of the various concepts discussed.
- The use of examples from the author's own experience in research. I have not hesitated to express my personal views on issues.
- Asking you to write in responses periodically throughout the text. This is particularly important since it provides an on-going opportunity for you to respond and be involved in the process of research and to evaluate your responses.
- Including my own reactions so that you may compare your responses to my comments. You can, of course, skip those portions where you are asked to respond, but in doing so, you will deprive yourself of what is probably the most meaningful learning experience the book provides. You will also deprive yourself of the opportunity to compare your thinking with mine and to discover that in some instances yours may be better. Students in "try out" classes reported this to be one of the most valuable features of the book. Most said they looked ahead only occasionally. Sometimes, in giving my responses, I have included new information, that is, information you were not given before making your response. This has been done deliberately as a way of extending your learning and to discourage the tendency to look for oversimplified "correct" answers.
- Asking you throughout the book to continue to develop an initial problem of your own choice, thus tying the concepts about which you are learning to a problem of interest to you.

vii

By the end of the book, if you have completed these sections, you will have, in effect, written a research proposal and reported on a pilot study.

Special mention needs to be made of the place of statistics in this book. It is my view that the place of statistics in an introductory course is: (a) to help the student interpret information he has collected; and (b) to provide an understanding of some of the important concepts and ideas used in statistical reasoning. Therefore, detailed computation and mastery of complex statistical ideas have not been included. Statistics are an extremely useful tool for making sense of data and for simplifying some important concepts. It is in this way that they are treated in this book.

There is one feature of the research process that cannot be adequately handled in any text. In reality, research does not consist of going through a series of defined steps, but rather is a continuing dynamic process in which one aspect of planning a study interacts with others. For example, thinking through the issue of what subjects to use may change the direction of the entire study. In a book, however, one must treat things in some order. The particular ordering of this text is by no means the only one possible; I think you will find it helpful if you keep this necessary artificiality in mind.

It is my conviction that everyone involved in the educational process should have an understanding of some basic, essential research concepts. I do not agree that educational research should remain the exclusive province of a relatively small group of experts. Even those who say they see no value in research are increasingly affected by it as our society continues to invest time and money in finding better solutions to continuing problems. School personnel are frequently asked to participate in research and to accept policies on the grounds that "research has shown . . . ." Surely, one ought, at the very least, to know what questions to ask about such research. There is no better way to become informed than to get involved in the process.

Hopefully, you are, or will become sufficiently interested to want to learn more about the research process. In any case, you will have barely scratched the surface with this book. If successful, it will provide a basic skeleton to which the richness of detail can be added as needed.

To the Student:

This book has been developed in close collaboration with students in the author's research classes. We would very much like to obtain reactions from a broader range of student users. We are particularly interested in *your* opinion about the somewhat novel ideas that have been incorporated into this book.

Your reactions will be given serious consideration and will have a direct effect on future revisions. Please look over the response form in the back of the book now so that you can keep the questions in mind as you use the text. The research process can be an exciting intellectual adventure. I hope that this book can help make it so for you.

To the Instructor:

This book has two purposes: The first is to help introduce the process of doing educational research to the student in such a way that it is an exciting and interesting adventure. It is, I think, a fact that unfortunately most current texts do not facilitate this purpose for a great many students who take the introductory course in research methods in education. The second purpose is to foster the development of basic concepts and skills in students to the point that they can, when the occasion requires, evaluate research perceptively and have at least a skeleton of the research process to which the meat may be added when needed. When these two purposes appear to conflict, as when the author was tempted to go into elaborate detail on certain methodological issues, he forced himself to give priority to the former.

This book may be used either as a basic text or as a supplementary text. It provides for easy checking on student progress through the fill-in student responses, especially those sections applying to the student's own research plan.

Most instructors will wish to go into greater depth either in terms of the particular interests and needs of students or in terms of areas that their own interest or perspective indicates should be strengthened. Some instructors may wish to use a second, more traditional text and assign the chapters in it to parallel those in this book.

If the book is assigned as out-of-class work, student responses can be evaluated and used as the basis for discussion in individual conferences or in class. An alternative is to have students fill in responses in class.

It is a pleasure to thank the following colleagues for their review and many suggestions: Sam Levine; Gabe Della-Piana; and Jack Fraenkel, who also used the earlier versions in his classes and served as editor. I am much indebted to the students who used the book, made many suggestions for improvement, and encouraged me that I was on the right track.

Contents

1. Developing the Research Problem
   or "How to Get Started"   1

   Introduction   1
   Posing the Question   2
   Feasibility   3
   Clarification   7
   Background Reading   17
   Justification   22
   Hypothesis Formation   26
   Summary   34
   References for Further Reading   35

2. Instrumentation
   or "How to Get a Handle on It"   36

   Introduction   36
   Ratings   37
   Reliability and Validity   45
   The Observation Record   48
   The Structured Interview   53
   Ability Tests   59
   Projective Tests   72
   Summary   82
   References for Further Reading   82

3. Sampling
   or "Where Do the Findings Apply?"   84

   Introduction   84
   Generalizing   86
   Examples of Sampling   93
   Summary   109
   References for Further Reading   110

4. Procedures
   or "How to Avoid Kidding Yourself"   111

   Introduction   111
   Contamination   117
   Sources of Bias   126

xii   Contents

Identification of Bias   129
Summary   157
References for Further Reading   157

5.   Interpretation of Data
        or "How to Make Sense Out of Information"   158

Introduction   158
Single Group Designs   158
Multiple Group Designs   168
Statistical Inference   186
Summary   203
References for Further Reading   204

6.   Critiquing Research Reports
        or "How to Separate the Wheat from the Chaff"   205

Introduction   205
Criteria for Evaluating Research Reports   205
Critiquing Research Reports   210
Proposal   231
Summary   243
References for Further Reading   244

Glossary-Index   245

Student Questionnaire   247

Developing the Research Problem
or "How to Get Started"

INTRODUCTION

Since the intent of this book is to involve you in the research *process* as quickly as possible, this introduction will be brief. The topics discussed below are treated in greater depth in the references listed at the end of this chapter.

"Educational research" is usually justified by citing the advances made by the scientific method in other fields, implying that the same approach can bear similar fruit in education. The weaknesses of other ways of knowing—such as intuition, common sense, tradition, and personal experience—are elaborated and the superiority of objective science triumphantly declared. I think that it is sufficient to say that the scientific method, applied to education, provides us with a way of knowing that often is illuminating and, in its own way, potentially exciting.

There are various systems for classifying research studies by type—descriptive, predictive, survey, etc. Although useful for many purposes, these classifications have, with a few exceptions, been omitted as not essential to this presentation. The first exception is that research, as treated in this book, involves the collection of information (data) at first hand. This is often referred to as empirical research. Thus, historical research is not included. The second exception is that the unique features of experimental studies are treated at some length (in chapter four).

The findings of a basic research study:
- should apply to a great many people and/or situations;
- should be related to many other studies and/or theories;
- need not have obvious or immediate implications for practice.

Example: A study of the relative contribution of heredity and environment to aggressive behavior in children in school.

In contrast, the findings of an applied research study:
- are applicable to a specific group of people in a specific situation (they may or may not apply elsewhere);
- need not relate to a broader field of knowledge or to other research;
- have immediate and obvious implications for practice.

Example: A study of opinions of the faculty at San Francisco State University toward collective bargaining.

Many studies, of course, do not fit neatly into either category but fall on a continuum between these extremes.

Enough of background. Let's begin involving you in the process of educational research. The aim is to equip you to develop a plan for a study that you could (perhaps will) actually carry out. In doing so, we will think through a series of steps that are in a particular sequence only because a book is "linear," to use McLuhan's term. You should expect to modify earlier steps as you proceed. At the completion of this chapter, you will have developed a research hypothesis, clarified your terms, and justified your proposed study. You will have examined the feasibility of your proposed study and will have conducted a small-scale literature search.

POSING THE QUESTION

The first step in doing a research study is to state the problem to be investigated. Many questions are being asked in relation to our schools today. Think about a question you would like to investigate. Choose one that interests you and is related to your field of interest. In doing this, keep in mind one additional factor—it is essential that the question you select be within your own educational setting and one for which you will be able to collect data. Educational research need not always involve raw data, but you will learn more about the total research process if you carry it through in its entirety.

As you think about a question, then, you should try to determine if it would be feasible for you to collect enough information to provide at least a partial answer to your question. Also, try to formulate a question that will involve you in the process of collecting data, rather than simply compiling data from existing records. The former will provide a much richer experience for you. For example, a study that requires only the examination of school records does not give you experience in locating, evaluating, and/or developing techniques for data collection.

FEASIBILITY

My emphasis on feasibility does not mean that we should select for study only that which seems easy or obvious. The focus, however, is on your involvement in the process—hence the stress on avoiding the frustration of too many dead ends.

Listed below is a series of questions. Think of a way that *you* could collect information (from colleagues, students, friends, etc.) that would help to answer the question. Please respond to each of the questions in the space provided. Indicate "yes" or "no" as to whether or not *you* could collect data for each question. If your answer is "yes," briefly state how you would go about your collection; if you answer "no," briefly explain why you could not. You will notice that some of the questions contain ambiguous terms and are stated rather poorly. Don't let this disturb you—this is how most research questions *begin*. Further, although it is impossible to be precise about feasibility until terms are defined, this is an *initial* exploration to help you select a question of your own that is feasible for you to investigate. The first question was investigated as a class project in one of my research classes and will be used to provide examples throughout the book. As you will see as we proceed, the study is not an example of first rate research. However, I think you will learn more from it than from a highly sophisticated example.

Question 1. Does the open classroom work?

Could you collect data? Yes _____   No _____

How? Or why not? _____

_____

_____

Question 2. How do students feel about special classes for the educationally handicapped?

Could you collect data? Yes _____   No _____

How? Or why not? _____

_____

_____

_____

Question 3. Do children in the second grade like school?

Could you collect data? Yes _____ No _____

How? Or why not? _____

_____

_____

_____

Question 4. Does a counselor have to like his counselees?

Could you collect data? Yes _____ No _____

How? Or why not? _____

_____

_____

_____

Check your "yes" and "no" explanations against the comments provided on page 6.

AUTHOR'S COMMENTS

*"Does the open classroom work?" To collect information on
this question, you need access to people who have had experience
with the open classroom. If there are examples of this approach
in your school community, you might be able to observe in the
classroom, talk to students, or administer a questionnaire or
test. Or you may have access to an open classroom outside your
community. You may be able to think of a way to assess the
opinions of people who have had contact with this teaching approach. Without access, it is difficult to see how you might
investigate this question. This is not to say that this or any
of the other questions is a very researchable one as stated, but
for our purpose the feasibility question must be met first.*

*"How do students feel about special classes for the educa-
tionally handicapped?" To investigate this question, you would
need access to individuals (preferably students) who have some
experience with these classes.*

*"Do children in the second grade like school?" Although
there may be many difficulties in studying this question, many
teachers have some access to second graders or their parents.
Consequently, the question of feasibility would probably be
answered "yes."*

*"Does a counselor have to like his counselees?" This ques-
tion requires access to a group of either counselors or counselees, or others who are familiar with the therapeutic process.*

At this point, please write the question that you would
like to investigate and, very briefly, describe your general approach for collecting information (data).

Your question: _____

_____

_____

How would the data be collected? _____

_____

_____

_____

_____

CLARIFICATION

The question as you have stated it may be perfectly clear
to you and to others. Frequently, however, this is not the
case. Look again at the four previous examples. In the first
example, the term *open classroom* may seem quite straightforward.
However, those who are acquainted with this approach probably
will agree that the term needs clarification. If we ask, "What
are the essential characteristics of the open classroom?" we
discover how difficult it is to specify them. Descriptions of
the open classroom usually suggest that the child has a wide
choice of activities and that the teacher is a resource person
rather than a director of activities. However, such descriptions also point out that great variation in these characteristics and others exists from classroom to classroom and from
school to school (such as the degree of total school and community involvement, and the amount of materials available).
Thus, what initially may appear to be a straightforward description on closer examination is shown to be much more complex.

This is true of many current educational concepts and meth-
odologies. Although such ambiguity is valuable for certain purposes, it represents a problem to the investigator of a research
question. If he is to examine a particular teaching method, he
needs to know precisely what he is to study. The investigator
has no choice but to try to be more specific about his terms.
In doing so, he may gain a much clearer picture of how to proceed; even the nature of the investigation may change in a
rather fundamental way.

The investigator who wishes to clarify the phrase *open
classroom* has essentially two alternatives. The first is to
define the concept through what is often referred to as the
"dictionary" or "literary" approach. We might try to describe
as fully as possible the essential characteristics of the open
classroom, including examples of classrooms that have these
characteristics. This time-honored approach, however, has its
limitations, as any semanticist will attest. The two characteristics that have been suggested above as common to all open
classrooms also contain ambiguous words. For example, what is
meant by "choice" and how much is "a wide choice"? What does a
teacher actually *do* when acting as a "resource"?

Operational definitions, the second method of clarification, also require words, but they specify the operations or
actions needed to identify the term being defined. Here are
three possible operational definitions of the open classroom:
(1) any classroom identified by the teacher or principal as
using the open classroom method; (2) any classroom identified
as an open classroom by such recognized experts as H. Kohl or
J. Featherstone; and (3) any classroom judged to possess the

following attributes by an observer spending one day in the classroom: no more than three children working with the same materials at the same time; teacher never spending more than twenty minutes per day addressing the class as a group; and at least one-third of classroom objects having been made by children.

These may be quite unsatisfactory definitions of the open classroom. They are, however, considerably more specific than those used earlier. Armed with one or more of these definitions (and the necessary facilities), you could decide quickly whether or not a particular classroom matched your definition and, hence, whether or not it could be included in your study.

When we ask, "Does the open classroom work?" what do we mean by "work"? Does "work" mean "results in increased academic proficiency?" Perhaps it means "results in happier children" or "makes life easier for teachers," or "costs less money." Maybe the researchers mean all of these things and more. In any case, the meaning is not clear. In the class project (investigating this question) "work" was eventually defined as meaning "results in higher motivation," which also requires still more clarification. Here is the way one student defined "higher motivation": "A productive type of activity. A curiosity to learn more about or to be occupied by an observable person or object." Another defined it as: "Something that incites the organism to action or that sustains and gives direction to action once the organism has been aroused."

What differences between the two definitions do you see?

_____

_____

_____

_____

_____

AUTHOR'S COMMENTS

The second definition is less ambiguous. "Inciting to action" and "sustaining and giving direction to action" are less ambiguous than "curiosity," "productive," and "occupied by." If you apply each definition to another person's behavior, I think you will agree. Further clarity might result from an operational definition such as: A class is highly motivated when the energy output of the class as a whole is judged high (as compared to other classes) by two independent observers observing for eight thirty-minute periods; and the amount of tangible work produced during these same periods is judged high by two different, independent judges.

Identify and clarify any ambiguous terms in the following examples. Try to include at least a few operational definitions.

Question 2: How do students feel about special classes for the educationally handicapped?

Clarify ambiguous terms: _____

_____

_____

_____

_____

_____

_____

Question 3: Do children in the second grade like school?

Clarify ambiguous terms: _____

_____

_____

_____

_____

11 Clarification

_____

_____

_____

_____

Question 4: Does a counselor have to like his counselees?

Clarify ambiguous terms: _____

_____

_____

_____

_____

_____

_____

_____

AUTHOR'S COMMENTS

"How do students feel about special classes for the educationally handicapped?"   The first term needing clarification is students.   *What age group is involved?   Are public or private schools or both included?   Are students throughout the nation or in only a particular community included?   Is the term meant to include students who are not in special classes as well as those who are?*

The phrase "feel about" is extremely ambiguous.   Does it mean opinions or emotional reactions?   Does it mean "students" are "in touch" (a literal but clearly unintended meaning)?   It should be noted that the term feelings, *although widely used in education today, is extremely difficult to define.   The question is likely directed toward student opinions about various aspects of special programs.*

Special classes *and* educationally handicapped *also must be further clarified.   The legal definition in California of an educationally handicapped student is a minor who, by reason of marked learning or behavioral disorders, is unable to adapt to a normal classroom situation.   The disorder must be associated with a neurological handicap or an emotional disturbance and must not be due to mental retardation, cultural deprivation, or foreign language problems.   Note that this legal definition contains such ambiguous terms as "marked learning disorders," which easily lend themselves to a wide variety of interpretations. (This is equally true of terms like* cultural deprivation, *which are not only ambiguous but often offensive to members of ethnic minorities to whom they are frequently applied.)*

"Do second graders like school?"   The major complication here is the word like.   *Possible operational definitions of* like *in this context include:*

a) when questioned verbally, students state that they enjoy school;

b) when observed in school, students show a higher frequency of smiling and laughing behavior than of frowning and crying behavior;

c) when offered the option of attending school or staying at home, students elect to attend school;

d) when looking at a series of pictures depicting both pleasurable and unpleasurable reactions of school children in school and asked, "Which one of these pictures is you?", student chooses a preponderance of pleasurable pictures.

"Does a counselor have to like his counselees?"   This question requires clarification of who is to be considered a counselor for the purposes of the study: high school counselor; elementary school counselor; rehabilitation counselor; mental health worker; or a combination of these.   The term like *also*

must be clarified. Furthermore, the question implies some
assessment of the effects of liking or not liking; in other
words, what is meant by have to?

Returning to the question that you stated on page 6, see
whether there are any terms that need clarification. In the
spaces below list both the terms and the ways in which you propose to clarify them, using both operational and dictionary
definitions.

Words   Definitions

_____   _____

                               _____

_____   _____

                               _____

_____   _____

                               _____

_____   _____

                               _____

It is important now to verify your work by collecting some
outside information. Here is an exercise that will enable you
to check the clarity of your terms. Identify two or three individuals who know something about the field of education. Follow
the procedures described below with each of them.
Present your question exactly as stated on page 6, explaining that you are thinking of investigating this question. Ask
your respondent if he understands what you want to investigate
and if he finds the question in any way confusing. Write the
responses in the spaces provided. If there are any questions
your respondent asks in order to clarify your question, write
these down also. Now remove your question from view and ask
your respondent to rephrase it; record all responses to this
question.

Respondent 1

Your question: _____

_____

Respondent's reaction: _____

_____

_____

_____

Respondent's restatement of the question: _____

_____

_____

_____

Present your definitions. Ask if they are clear. Then ask
if what you intend to do is clear, if there are any questions,
and if he has any suggestions for gathering information.

Your definitions: _____

_____

_____

Respondent's reaction: _____

_____

_____

Respondent's suggestions for gathering information (e.g.,
what kind of information would be relevant?): _____

_____

_____

15 Clarification

_____

_____

Respondent 2
Present your question.

Your question: _____

Respondent's reaction: _____

_____

_____

_____

Respondent's restatement of the question: _____

_____

_____

_____

Present your definitions.

Your definitions: _____

_____

_____

_____

Respondent's reaction: _____

_____

_____

_____

Respondent's suggestions for gathering information: _____

_____

_____

_____

_____

    Summarize the responses that you obtained. Do the re-
sponses demonstrate a clear understanding of your question? It
is my hunch that there will have been some need for clarification. Perhaps you discovered that your question meant something
quite different to your respondents than it meant to you. Consequently, you may wish to further revise your question and definitions and repeat this exercise again with different people.

Summary of responses: _____

_____

_____

_____

_____

_____

_____

    Using the information you have gained from the exercise
with your respondents, rewrite your question in the clearest
possible manner. Include definitions of terms where necessary.

Rewritten question: _____

_____

_____

_____

_____

_____

BACKGROUND READING

This is an appropriate time for some preliminary reading on your question. When planning a study, one should be familiar with pertinent literature. Although a detailed literature review is not essential for our purposes, you should become familiar with how to locate the appropriate references. In the next exercise, you will spend some time digging into the literature to find out what has been written pertinent to your question. A university library is your best resource; but if one is not available, the public library will be adequate. Try to locate at least four pertinent references, at least two of which are research reports that present data, and summarize them using the following model:

> Walberg, H. J., and Thomas, S. C. "Open Education: An Operational Definition and Validation in Great Britain and United States." *American Educational Research Journal* 9 (1972): 197-216.

The purpose of this article is to describe the development of an observation scale and a teacher questionnaire for assessing the degree of "openness" of a given elementary classroom. Items were written within each of eight "themes" obtained from available literature and reviewed by a panel of authorities.

The resulting instruments were used in approximately twenty classrooms for each of three types: British open, American open, and American traditional. The classrooms were identified by reputation and personal knowledge. Approximately equal numbers of lower and middle socioeconomic level classrooms were included.

Results showed that overall assessments obtained with the two different instruments (observation and questionnaire) agreed quite highly. Differences between the open and traditional classrooms were much greater than those between socioeconomic levels or between countries.

There aren't any sure-fire rules to follow when locating research studies on a particular topic. You should, however, be familiar with some of the available resources. A useful—though not exhaustive—list of these sources follows.

Basic References in the Social Sciences

White, C. M., et al. *Sources of Information in the Social Sciences*. Totowa, N.J.: Bedminister, 1964.
Berelson, B., Stiener, G. *Human Behavior—An Inventory of Scientific Findings*. New York, N.Y.: Harcourt Brace Jovanovich, 1964.
International Encyclopedia of the Social Sciences. New York, N.Y.: MacMillan, 1968.
Lindzey, G., ed. *Handbook of Social Psychology*. Reading, Mass.: Addison-Wesley, 1954.
Mussen, P. H., ed. *Handbook of Research Methods in Child Development*. New York, N.Y.: Wiley, 1960.

Guides to Educational Literature

Burke, A. J., Burke, M. A. *Documentation in Education*. 5th ed. New York, N.Y.: Teachers College Press, 1967.
Manheim, T., et al. *Sources in Educational Research*. Detroit: Wayne State University Press, 1969.

Basic References in Education

Buros, O. K. *The Seventh Mental Measurements Yearbook*. Highland Park, N.J.: Gryphon Press, 1972.
Buros, O. K. *Personality Tests and Reviews*. Highland Park, N.J.: Gryphon Press, 1970.
Buros, O. K. *Reading Tests and Reviews*. Highland Park, N.J.: Gryphon Press, 1968.
Ebel, R. L., et al. *Encyclopedia of Educational Research*. 4th ed. New York, N.Y.: Prentice-Hall, 1969.
Gage, N. *Handbook of Research on Teaching*. Chicago: Rand McNally, 1963.
Good, C. V. *Dictionary of Education*. 2d ed. New York, N.Y.: McGraw-Hill, 1959.
Smith, E. W. *The Educators Encyclopedia*. Englewood Cliffs, N.J.: Prentice-Hall, 1961.
Travers, R. M. W., ed. *Second Handbook of Research and Teaching*. Chicago: Rand McNally, 1972.

Guides to Current Literature

Education Index. New York, N.Y.: H. W. Wilson, 1932 to present.
Current Index to Journals in Education. New York, N.Y.: CCM Information Sciences, 1969 to present (monthly, contains abstracts).

Dissertation Abstracts.   Ann Arbor, Mich.: University Micro-
   films.
Psychological Abstracts.   Lancaster, Pa.: American Psychological
   Association, 1927 to present (monthly, six-month indexes).
Research in Education.   Washington, D.C.: Government Printing
   Office, 1967 to present (monthly, contains abstracts of USOE
   and other projects; ERIC).
Sociological Abstracts.   Brooklyn, N.Y.: Sociological Abstracts,
   Inc.

   ## *Annual Reviews*

Annual Phi Delta Kappa Symposium on Educational Research
Annual Review of Information Science and Technology
Annual Review of Psychology
Annual Review of Sociology
Association for Supervision and Curriculum Development Yearbook
National Council for the Social Studies Yearbook
National Society for the Study of Education Yearbook

   ## *Major Journals*

American Educational Research Journal
American Journal of Mental Deficiency
Behavior Research and Therapy
Child Development
The Crippled Child
Educational and Psychological Measurement
Harvard Educational Review
International Journal for the Education of the Blind
Journal of Applied Psychology
Journal of Counseling Psychology
Journal of Educational Psychology
Journal of Communication Disorders
Journal of Educational Research
Journal of Exceptional Children
Journal of Experimental Child Psychology
Journal of Experimental Education
Journal of Learning Disabilities
Journal of Research and Development in Education
Journal of Speech and Hearing Disorders
Journal of Speech and Hearing Research
Journal of Special Education
Journal of Teacher Education
Personnel and Guidance Journal
Phi Delta Kappan

Psychological Review
Rehabilitation Counseling Bulletin
Report on the Education of the Disadvantaged
Review of Educational Research
Social Education
Teachers College Record
Vocational Guidance Quarterly

Most of these references can be found in any university library. The card catalog and the library staff frequently can be of great help in locating references on a particular topic. Make an effort to locate at least one item within each of the preceding categories and spend some time familiarizing yourself with each.

Summary of reference 1: _____

_____

_____

_____

_____

_____

_____

_____

_____

_____

Summary of reference 2: _____

_____

_____

_____

_____

_____

_____

_____

_____

_____

_____

_____

Summary of reference 3: _____

_____

_____

_____

_____

_____

_____

_____

_____

_____

Summary of reference 4: _____

_____

_____

_____

_____

_____

_____

_____

_____

_____

_____

_____

Has this reading affected your thinking in such a way that you wish to change your original question and/or your definitions? If so, please state your revisions:

_____

_____

_____

_____

_____

_____

_____

JUSTIFICATION

Returning to your question, which should be in a clear and understandable form, let's ask, "What is the purpose of this study?" Presumably your question is of interest to you, since those were the instructions given when you formulated the question. Is this sufficient justification for an investigation? To some people, particularly to those dedicated to the pursuit of truth, the answer is a clear "yes." Any question that anyone sincerely wants to answer is worth investigating. It is important, however, that you practice justifying your question beyond this personal sense. When one considers the resources expended in educational research, it is easy to appreciate the point of view that some useful outcome or payoff should be forthcoming. The investment of oneself and others, of money, and of materials

should contribute to either practical or general knowledge.
Generally speaking, the research effort does not warrant investigation based only on personal curiosity. Furthermore, there
is ample reason to question the "purely curious" motive on psychological grounds. Most questions have some degree of hidden
motivation behind them; and for the sake of credibility, these
reasons should be made explicit.

One of the most difficult issues in research is deciding
the merits of a research question. Given the many questions
that could be investigated, which ones are likely to be most
fruitful in advancing knowledge or improving practice?

Write a defense of your question. That is to say, why
would it be important to try to answer your question, other
than because you are personally interested in doing so? Does
the question relate to current theories in the field? Does it
have implications for classroom practice or administrative decision making, or for program planning? Is there a clear issue
that can be illuminated by the study? It may be helpful to pre-
tend for the moment that you are in a position of wanting to
solicit funds to help you investigate the question. A granting
agency or individual is almost certain to ask you to justify
your investigation. Write a carefully thought-out justification
for your question.

Justification: _____

_____

_____

_____

_____

_____

One example of a student's justification for the open
classroom study follows:

The general purpose of this research is to add knowledge to the field of education at this time when classroom
freedom is a cornerstone of today's educational revolution.
Leonard, Holt, and Kohl have suggested that the strictly
structured, teacher-directed classroom may impede the
learning process. It is this controversial thesis, coupled
with an onslaught of programmed learning materials, that
has provoked many teachers and administrators to modify
their classroom structure in hopes of achieving greater

educational gains for their students. While reformers have
written convincingly from a psychological point of view
that students will be more highly motivated to learn in a
less structured setting, these reformers have not offered
data to support their thesis. If educators are to jump
safely on the open classroom bandwagon, they should have
information of the type this project will provide.

Another student wrote:

Education of children in elementary schools has always
been a controversial issue among parents and teachers.
There are various ideas regarding the type of setting that
would be a constructive learning situation for children.
One such setting that we feel is motivating for children is
the open classroom.

Another student:

The purpose is to research open classrooms and structured classrooms and to discover in which setting more student motivation takes place.

Compare these statements and list as many differences as
you can (other than length). _____

_____

_____

_____

_____

If you were in a position to approve (or fund) a study of
the open classroom, which of the three preceding justifications
do you feel would most likely result in your approval? Why?

_____

_____

_____

_____

_____

_____

As you compare *your* question and its justification with those presented above, what similarities and differences do you notice?

Similarities: _____

_____

_____

_____

_____

Differences: _____

_____

_____

_____

_____

AUTHOR'S COMMENTS

My reactions to the three statements are as follows: The third statement is a description of what is to be done. It contains no justification beyond the implication that discovery is a sufficient purpose in itself. The second statement gives some perspective on the study, but remains very general and fails to indicate how the study results might be used. The first statement seems to me to be a good one. It places the study in a context of both theoretical and practical work, indicates its importance at this time, and implies how the results can be used. The latter could be spelled out in even more detail.

Is there any position or point of view expressed above that you could use as additional justification for the question you have proposed?

Additional justification: _____

_____

_____

_____

_____

_____

HYPOTHESIS FORMATION

The essence of *hypothesis stating* is simply that a prediction is made regarding the possible outcomes of a study. Hypothesis stating is an extremely powerful technique, but it can lead to some problems. As we explore this procedure, I will attempt to deal with some of the controversy surrounding it. Returning to our example questions, let us now restate them as hypotheses.

Question 1 was originally stated as, "Does the open classroom work?" Recasting this into a hypothesis, we could say, "The open classroom does (or does not) work." Question 2, "How do students feel about special classes for the educationally handicapped?" could lead to a number of hypotheses: for example, "Students feel that special classes for the educationally handicapped constitute social stigma," or "Students feel that the special classes for educationally handicapped are of assistance

in improving academic skill."   Question 3, "Do children in the
second grade like school?" could lend itself to the hypothesis
that "Children in the second grade do (or do not) like school."
Question 4, "Does a counselor have to like his counselees?"
leads to the hypothesis that "Counselors do (or do not) have to
like their counselees."

What are the advantages of stating hypotheses? First, it
forces us to think more deeply about the possible outcomes of a
study. It is usually more difficult to state a hypothesis than
to ask a question. Stating a hypothesis in relation to a question can lead to a much more sophisticated understanding of what
is implied by the question. Often, as in the case of our example question 2, a choice of hypotheses forces us to look more
closely at what we actually want to investigate.

Let's return to example question 1. Originally stated it
was, "Does the open classroom work?" Subsequently, it was revised to: "Does the open classroom result in higher student
motivation?" (p. 8). We can now state a hypothesis: "The open
classroom does result in higher student motivation." Stating
the hypothesis leads us to examine why we would make such a
prediction. To do so, we need to consider many aspects of the
open classroom, its advantages and disadvantages, and then arrive at a prediction based on this accumulated knowledge. Because we cannot know for certain beforehand what the collected
data or information will show, we are taking a risk in making a
prediction. Therefore, we should be impressed if the findings
actually turn out as we predicted.

Further, stating a hypothesis should push us to extend our
thinking and stimulate us to begin thinking of ways to test it.
For example, it seems obvious that the testing of this hypothesis requires that we compare the open classroom to other teaching methods. Otherwise, there is no way to assess if higher
motivation is due to the teaching method used.

A second advantage of stating hypotheses concerns a philosophy of science. The rationale is as follows: If one is attempting to build a body of knowledge in addition to answering
a specific question, then stating hypotheses is a good strategy
because it enables one to make specific predictions based on
prior evidence or theory. If these predictions are borne out,
the entire procedure gains both in validity and efficiency.
These factors are of great concern in building a science. A
classic example is Einstein's theories that led to a great many
predictions or hypotheses. As these were verified, they not
only were useful in their own right, but gave increasing confidence in the ideas that had generated them.

In our example of the open classroom, there is no clear-cut
theory on which one can rely at this time. However, there are
general theories of behavior that are pertinent to our example.

Verification of our hypothesis would tend to support the theories that emphasize reliance on individual motivation rather than external controls.

The disadvantages of hypothesis stating are twofold. First, it may lead to a conscious or unconscious bias. Once the investigator has stated his hypothesis, he may be tempted to arrange the procedures or manipulate the data in such a way as to force the desired outcome. Should this occur, science has a built in protection in that studies may be repeated and findings verified. In practice, however, educational research studies are seldom repeated so this protection is somewhat illusory. We must assume that the researcher is intellectually honest. Any study should be subject to public inspection; in the past, this has sometimes revealed such inadequacies of method that the reported results were highly suspect. Unfortunately, a dishonest investigator stands a good chance of getting away with his deception. Why would one deliberately distort a study? Professional recognition and, sometimes, financial rewards accrue to the investigator who publishes important results.

Assuming the researcher is honest, his commitment to a hypothesis may result in distortions that are unintentional and unconscious. However, it seems unlikely that a researcher in the field of education is ever totally disinterested in the outcome of a study. Therefore, his attitudes or knowledge probably favor a particular result. If this is the case, it would seem desirable that these predilictions be stated, as in a hypothesis, so they are clear to the reader and so the investigator can take steps to insure an unbiased study.

The second disadvantage, frequently cited by behavior modification enthusiasts, is that focusing attention on a hypothesis may prevent the researcher from observing other phenomena that might be more important to study. For example, studying the impact of the open classroom on motivation may cause the researcher to overlook its effect on such characteristics as sextyping or decision making, which might be obvious to the sensitive observer who is more open to a variety of phenomena. Most educational research, however, has suffered more from lack of clarity than from lack of sensitive observation.

The next exercise asks you to restate your question in terms of a hypothesis. In other words, make a prediction about the answer to your question which will be provided by your data. In stating your hypothesis, avoid value terms (such as "should" or "ought") and variations of "can," because such words lead to unverifiable hypotheses. Research cannot determine what should be or what is ultimately possible.

Your hypothesis: _____

_____

_____

_____

_____

The next task is to develop a more sophisticated hypothesis.
Virtually all important hypotheses concerning education ask
about relationships, particularly when the intent is to use such
information either to support present procedures or to discover
better methods for doing things. This can be illustrated by
looking once again at our four original questions.

Question 1 stated as a hypothesis would be, "The open
classroom results in higher student motivation." This clearly
involves a comparison of the open classroom with something else
so that the real question is whether or not students experiencing the open classroom are more highly motivated than students in other classrooms. The relationship is between motivation and teaching method.

In question 2, any of the hypotheses stated on page 26
implicitly compare special classes and some other kind of arrangement. Thus the relationship is between student feelings
and type of class. Suppose, for example, one of the hypotheses
is that students feel that special classes help them academically. Although this may be interesting and valuable to know,
it might be more valuable to know what similar students in regular classrooms say. If students in regular classes express more
favorable opinions about their learning, the initial finding
(special classes help academically) would be misleading.

In response to question 3, "Do children in second grade
like school?" most second graders may say they like school; but
aren't we primarily interested in their feelings about second
grade in relation to other things a second grader might do? For
instance, how does their liking for school compare to their
liking for T.V.? Or we may wish to compare to other grades: do
second graders express liking for school to a greater or lesser
extent than first graders? It is not my intent to suggest that
this hypothesis, as originally stated, was uninteresting or un-
important; rather, that it can be extended to become more powerful; that is, it may lead to more useful knowledge. Compare
the following hypotheses to each of the four original questions.
Don't they seem more informative, clear, and powerful?

Hypothesis 1: The greater the openness of the classroom,
the higher the students' motivation will be.

Hypothesis 2: Students with academic disabilities, defined as educationally handicapped, will have more negative attitudes about themselves if they are in special classes than if they are in regular classes.

Hypothesis 3: Second graders like school less than first graders but more than third graders.

Hypothesis 4: The more positive the counselor's reaction, the more the counselee will grow.

Notice that these hypotheses state a comparison or relationship between one thing and another. Thus, the more sophisticated hypothesis states a predicted relationship.

What is related to what in hypothesis 3? _____

_____

What is related to what in hypothesis 4? _____

_____

AUTHOR'S COMMENT

In hypothesis 3, liking for school is related to grade level (one to three). In hypothesis 4, positive reaction of counselor is related to counselee's growth.

All the hypotheses predict rather definitely that a certain outcome will take place. The findings of our study on the open classroom, it seems reasonable to say, will turn out in one of three ways: (1) We may discover that the open classroom does produce higher motivation. (2) The open classroom may make no difference at all. (3) The open classroom may produce lower motivation. Before the data are collected, however, there is no way of knowing what the results will be. If we choose the first or third option before looking at the data, we are stating a directional hypothesis; that is, we are stating how motivation is related to openness of the classroom.

Sometimes it is difficult to make such specific predictions. If you suspect that a relationship exists but have no basis for prediction, you cannot make a directional hypothesis. For example, you might expect that the degree of openness in a classroom is related to the students' motivation, but be uncertain as to how it specifically relates. You may feel that the relationship is important but be unable to predict whether open classrooms will have students with higher or lower motivation. It is quite possible to state hypotheses in this nondirectional form. Stated this way it would read, "The degree of openness in the classroom will be related to the degree of motivation of the students." Notice that in this case there is no prediction about high or low motivation, only that there will be a relationship.

Directional hypotheses are preferable to nondirectional hypotheses because they are more powerful when verified. In the example above, the nondirectional hypothesis predicts that the first *or* third outcome will occur. Suppose the results are consistent with the first outcome. Wouldn't you be more impressed if the hypothesis had predicted the first outcome ahead of time?

In this next exercise, try to state a nondirectional hypothesis that involves a relationship for questions 2, 3, and 4.

Question 2: _____

_____

_____

33 HYPOTHESIS FORMATION

Question 3: _____

_____

_____

Question 4: _____

_____

_____

AUTHOR'S COMMENTS

    Compare your hypotheses with the following examples: For question 2, "Students in special classes will differ from similar students not in special classes with respect to their self-concept." Question 3, "Second graders will differ from first and third graders in their liking for school." Question 4, "Positive reactions on the part of the counselor are related to expressed growth on the part of the counselee."

    The final exercise in this section, as you may expect, is to state your hypothesis in terms of a relationship. Try to formulate a directional hypothesis. However, a nondirectional hypothesis is acceptable provided that it states a relationship.

    Hypothesis: _____

_____

_____

_____

SUMMARY

    At this point, you have developed a hypothesis that is presumably *clear*, has been *justified* as worthy of investigation, and is *feasible* for you to investigate. Take time to review these topics (clarity, justification, feasibility) and their interrelations. You may want to revise certain of your earlier statements in order to make your hypothesis clear, feasible, and justified. When you are satisfied that your plan is adequate, you are ready to consider instrumentation. Instrumentation, the means to collecting information, is the topic of chapter two.

    The basic concepts considered in this chapter were:

Basic and applied research
Feasibility
Clarification
Dictionary definition
Operational definition
Literature sources
Justification
Hypothesis

REFERENCES FOR FURTHER READING

Borg, W. F. *Educational Research.* 2d ed. New York, N.Y.: David McKay, 1971. Chaps. 1, 2.

Engelhart, M. D. *Methods of Educational Research.* Chicago: Rand McNally, 1972. Chaps. 1, 2. 4.

Featherstone, J. *Schools Where Children Learn.* New York, N.Y.: Liveright, 1970.

Fox, D. J. *The Research Process in Education.* New York, N.Y.: Holt, Rinehart & Winston, 1969. Chaps. 1, 15, 16.

Good, C. V. *Essentials of Educational Research.* New York, N.Y.: Appleton-Century-Crofts, 1959. Chaps. 1, 2.

Helmstadter, G. C. *Research Concepts in Human Behavior.* New York, N.Y.: Appleton-Century-Crofts, 1970. Chap. 1.

Kaplan, A. *The Conduct of Inquiry.* San Francisco: Chandler, 1964. Chaps. 1, 2.

Kerlinger, F. N. *Foundations of Behavioral Research.* New York, N.Y.: Holt, Rinehart & Winston, 1964. Chaps. 1, 2.

Travers, R. M. W. *An Introduction to Educational Research.* 2d ed. New York, N.Y.: Holt, Rinehart & Winston, 1964. Chaps. 1, 2, 3.

2

Instrumentation
or "How to Get a Handle on It"

INTRODUCTION

What instruments can be used to obtain information to test our hypothesis? For many students, this is one of the most interesting parts of planning a study. It is, at the same time, one of the most important and sometimes difficult aspects of research. There are many tools that may be used to obtain information. In the following pages, we will look at some examples of the most widely used types of instruments.

At the end of this chapter you should be able to identify a variety of types of instruments and analyze specific instruments in terms of their value for a specific purpose. You will have begun the process of selecting or constructing instrumentation for your proposed study.

The following is a description of the process used by the research class that investigated the hypothesis: "The more open the classroom, the higher the student motivation." That process resulted in the development of two instruments: a *rating scale* and an *observation record*. As these instruments are described, the meaning of these terms should become clear. It is important to keep in mind that these instruments are the products of a particular group of people who worked on the problem. There are undoubtedly other ways to tackle this problem; perhaps you will think of a better way.

At the outset, it was clear that we needed ways of assessing the degree of openness and the level of student motivation within a particular classroom. Only by having a measurement of each of these attributes could we determine if a relationship existed between them. We began with openness and selected two commonly used measuring procedures. The first was direct observation in the classroom and the second was the asking of questions of students and teachers. Each member of the research class expanded on his knowledge of the open classroom by reading pertinent literature, talking with colleagues, or visiting classrooms purporting to be open.

Further input was obtained from two documents brought to class by students. One was a statement of intent on the part of a school district to move in the direction of openness; it indicated some specific changes that the district intended to make. The other document, although not concerned with our particular problem, listed examples of the kinds of things one could look for when observing in classrooms.

Next, each student was asked to make a list of specific things that could be taken as indicators of openness. These suggestions were pulled together and formed the basis for developing a useable instrument. The procedure involved committee work followed by review and discussion by the total class. The committee procedure was this: The class was divided into four committees, each to consolidate the lists that each class member had developed. As part of this process, some progress was made in defining the terms used. The resulting four lists were then duplicated for each class member. At a subsequent meeting, it was decided that each of the four committees would concern itself with certain groupings that seemed to emerge from the items. For example, a number of items seemed to have to do with the physical arrangement of the classroom, so this constituted one group. Table 2.1 shows the list of suggested indicators within each category. Each committee then attempted to refine and clarify the items within its particular category (categories).

As this process moved along, the question of the mechanics necessary in assessing these specific items arose. The instructor suggested that two instruments would be appropriate. The first would consist of a series of rating scales on which an observer would make a judgment as to the degree to which each indicator was present in the classroom. Other items would be better assessed by asking questions either of pupils or their teachers. Once the decision to use a rating system had been made, it was clear that for optimal use at least the ends of the scale had to be defined.

RATINGS

The next task was to convert the statements in table 2.1 to items for the rating scale. This was done by each committee with total class review. The resultant items are shown in table 2.2.

TABLE 2.1
INDICATORS OF CLASSROOM OPENNESS

Physical Environment: Are the desks in rows? Desks in study
centers? Specific learning centers for subjects? Are classes
ever held outdoors? In other parts of the outside community?
In the classroom, is there a general meeting area? Is there any
other type of furniture such as sofas, rocking chairs, over-
stuffed chairs, etc.? Are children free to move outside with no
adult present? How many adults are in the room? Paraprofessionals, teachers, volunteers, etc.? Multi-age grouping or
self-contained according to age level?

Curriculum: What amount of time does the teacher spend in planning? In evaluating? What type of planning does the teacher
use? Written lesson plans, behavioral objectives, etc.? Does
she have a list of overall objectives? How much time is spent
in academic curriculum? In arts and crafts? In social discussion, problem solving? Do children direct their own planning
or curriculum? Is there a contract system in effect? Is the
affective included in the curriculum? Are children taught to
express feelings? Are grades given?

Teacher-Pupil Relationships: Count times teacher gives direction
(vs. helping). Count student-initiated activity. Can children
leave the classroom on their own vs. ask permission or sign out?
Does the teacher help students individually, in small group
teaching, or total classroom teaching? Do students and teacher
evaluate together? Are class meetings teacher-directed or
student-directed? Do children make their own schedule? Do they
choose their own free time?

Materials: Are children assigned specific materials? How much
time is spent in workbooks? Are there manipulative materials?
Are children free to choose those materials and are they easily
accessible, or do children have to ask for them? Is the use of
materials directed by the teacher or students? Do children use
available books freely? Are there art materials freely available?

Social Environment: Children encouraged to help one another?
Tutor one another? Are children free to talk to one another all
the time? Part of the time? Never? Do children work alone, or
choose to work together? Do children group themselves, or are
they teacher-arranged? Do children share in room cleanup? How
many times does a teacher have to ask for quiet? Does physical
aggression occur between students frequently? Is aggression
handled by teacher or students directly? Does the child solve

the problem with guidance by the teacher, or does the teacher direct the solution?

Parent Participation: Are parents allowed in classrooms? Observers? Participants? Are parents free to enter school as they wish, or is there a formal procedure to go through? Are they allowed at all? Is there a volunteer parent-aide program? How many volunteers? Do they perform clerical or teaching tasks, mainly?

TABLE 2.2
RATING SCALE FOR CLASSROOM OPENNESS[1]

1. Students do not move without teacher permission	1 2 3 4 5	Children free to move in or out of the classroom without permission
2. All students working at the same task at the same time	1 2 3 4 5	Great variety of tasks being performed at the same time
3. Teacher is the only resource in the classroom	1 2 3 4 5	Several human resources (other than teacher) in classroom
4. Human resources are clerical or housekeeper aides to the teacher	1 2 3 4 5	Human resources interact with individual children and/or with small groups
5. Furniture is permanently arranged	1 2 3 4 5	Furniture is spontaneously arranged
6. Everyone works at his own desk	1 2 3 4 5	There are many floating study centers
7. Desks, tables, and chairs have a traditional arrangement	1 2 3 4 5	Complete variety of furniture: couch, rocking chair, rugs, pillows have a variety of arrangements
8. Students cannot interact with each other without direct permission from the teacher	1 2 3 4 5	Students are free to interact in any way with any others as they desire
9. Teacher initiates activity	1 2 3 4 5	Student initiates activity
10. Teacher teaches class as a group	1 2 3 4 5	Teacher works with small groups or individual students
11. Teacher formally addressed (Mrs. X; hand raised)	1 2 3 4 5	Teacher informally addressed (first name, nickname, no name)
12. Reprimands by punitive	1 2 3 4 5	No reprimands or only friendly reminders
13. No feelings verbally express	1 2 3 4 5	Much feeling is verbally expressed
14. Follow text closely	1 2 3 4 5	No formally prepared materials for class use

[1]In order to minimize the tendency for one rating to influence subsequent ratings the "desirable" pole should be sometimes 1, sometimes 5. In this example it is always 5 in order to simplify the presentation.

41 Ratings

Record any differences that you notice between the original
set of indicators (table 2.1) and the final rating form (table
2.2):

_____

_____

_____

_____

_____

_____

AUTHOR'S COMMENT

Only a few of the indicators in table 2.1 were converted directly into rating scale items (table 2.2). All items except 2 and 11 relate quite directly to one or more indicators. For example, item 1 encompasses two indicators: "Are children free to move outside with no adult present?" and "Can children leave the classroom on their own vs. ask permission or sign out?". However, the wording has in most cases changed in the transition. Items 2 and 11 do not relate to specific indicators, but emerged from the conversion process. The focus on observables eliminated many indicators, particularly under the heading of curriculum and parent participation.

The idea of developing questions to be asked of students and/or teachers was abandoned at this time because it lacked feasibility. The class did not have sufficient time to both observe and interview. It is not uncommon to have to omit desirable features of a study due to lack of feasibility. A more extensive study, of course, does not encounter the same difficulties as a class project.

Look back over the list of suggested indicators of openness in table 2.1, and determine which ones could be *better* assessed through use of interviews. Write down the specific indicator and whether you would assess this with interviews of students or teachers or both. Also state why you think that the interview approach would be superior to the classroom observation for that particular indicator.

Indicator	Who Is To Be Interviewed	Why Interview Is Superior To Observation
_____	_____	_____
_____	_____	_____
_____	_____	_____
_____	_____	_____
_____	_____	_____
_____	_____	_____

AUTHOR'S COMMENTS

Those items better assessed through interview would be those that: are difficult to observe directly, are within the province of knowledge of the respondent, and are likely to elicit straightforward replies. For example, students would best be asked:
"Are classes ever held outdoors?"
"Do they (students) choose free time?"
"Are children free to choose (manipulative) materials and are they easily accessible or do children have to ask for them?"
"Are children free to talk to one another?"
"Do children share in room cleanup?"

Teachers would best be asked:
"Is multi-age grouping or self-contained according to age level best?"
"What amount of time does teacher spend in planning?"
"Do students and teacher evaluate together?"
"Are children assigned specific materials?"
"Are parents free to enter school as they wish?"

You may wonder why it was necessary for the class to develop a measure of classroom openness rather than use an already available instrument. So far as we could determine, no appropriate instrument existed.[2] There is, of course, often an instrument available that does suit the needs of a particular study. The problem then becomes one of familiarizing oneself with the instrument and evaluating it in the context of the specific study. In many cases, however, one has to develop an instrument. There is no simple way of doing this. The development of a good instrument can be a very time-consuming process, in many cases requiring a good deal of specialized knowledge and a degree of talent. It is for these reasons that one makes use of instruments previously developed whenever feasible.

The term *instrument* refers to the device used in collecting information. Throughout this section, various forms of instruments (such as tests, rating scales, and questionnaires) will be discussed. Whatever the instrument, it is only useful when it provides the investigator with an index of the particular characteristic in question. In our example, the rating scale (instrument) will be useful in the open classroom study only to the extent that it gives us an index or reading on the degree of openness in a particular classroom.

---

[2] The report summarized on page 16 describing a similar approach to instrument development had not yet been published.

To obtain this index, one could simply add together the ratings in a particular classroom on each of the fourteen specific items. Thus, a classroom rated at the bottom of each item (score of 1) would receive a total of 14 points. A classroom rated at the top of each item (score of 5) would receive a total of 70 points (highest possible openness). This numerical score for a particular classroom is referred to as the *measurement* or score.

RELIABILITY AND VALIDITY

Two concepts that are extremely important in judging the value of an instrument are reliability and validity. *Reliability* is defined as the consistency of a measurement. *Validity* is the extent to which the obtained measurement actually provides us with the information we want. The question here is: Does the instrument measure what it is intended to measure?

If we used a yardstick to measure a desk and obtained different readings on each of three successive measures, we would conclude that our yardstick (as used) was not reliable (i.e., did not give consistent readings) and consequently of questionable value. In order to be useful, our instrument must provide us with measurements that have a degree of consistency appropriate to our purpose.

Lack of consistency may be caused by three things:

● First, how the instrument is used can create inconsistency. For example, desk measurements may be inconsistent due to incorrect reading by the person doing the measuring. This could be checked by having several persons do the measuring. In education, different observers might check each other's measurements of classroom behavior.

● Second, changes can be caused by passage of time. If someone cut our desk in half between measurements, this would clearly create inconsistency. In education, changes in observed behavior can be caused by maturation for example. This can be checked by comparing measurements obtained at different times.

● Third, change can be due to sampling of behavior. This source of inconsistency is relatively unique to behavioral science. It occurs because any measurement of human behavior uses indicators; it virtually never encompasses all behavior included in the characteristic of interest. For example, an algebra test must sample from the possible problems that could be given; and observers must look for certain indicators of openness even though there are undoubtedly others. This can be checked by comparing measurements using different indicators (or different test items).

If we were foolish enough to use our yardstick as an instrument for judging the degree of artistic merit in a desk, we would not obtain a valid measurement. That is, the measurement obtained (number of inches) is clearly not valid as an indicator of the characteristic in which we are interested (artistic merit). A less obvious example of the importance of validity concerns the widespread use of tests that require the student to read a passage and then answer questions about it. Several such passages with content in a particular field such as physical science are often used to provide a measure of a student's ability to comprehend material in the field. But for a poor reader, the test may not give a valid measure of his ability to comprehend the material.

There are two basic ways to evaluate validity: logical analysis and empirical evidence.

• Logical analysis: Does the measurement logically appear to measure the intended characteristic? For example, one can, on logical grounds, raise serious questions about the measurements obtained by giving an IQ test in English to recent immigrants from Mexico.

• Empirical evidence: Does the measurement agree with measurements obtained with different instruments that are also intended to measure the same characteristic?

Applying the concepts of reliability and validity to our rating scale, we can ask several questions. First, "To what extent do different observers watching the same classroom at the same time give the same ratings?" This can be investigated by having two observers observe independently and compare their results. However, this is only a part of the matter of reliability; the observers may agree at the same time, but give very different ratings at different times. To investigate this issue, one can observe a classroom a number of times and compare the extent to which ratings are similar. Reliable measurements of classroom characteristics can rarely be obtained from a single visit. Researchers generally agree that nine to twelve observation periods are required.

The problem of empirical validity is a bit more complex. It is necessary to obtain other assessments of the degree of openness for each classroom and compare the assessments with our ratings. One might question students and see whether their answers agree with our ratings as to which classrooms are the most open. If they do agree, both approaches are probably getting at the same thing. If they do not agree, then one or both may not be giving us valid information. At this point we would need further data, preferably on additional instruments, in order to evaluate the validity of our ratings.

What are some other ways that we might try to collect information on each classroom and compare it to the ratings to get further data on the validity of our measurements?

_____

_____

_____

_____

_____

_____

_____

AUTHOR'S COMMENTS

Some examples of validation procedures follow:
Obtain parents' opinions about the degree of openness through some form of question asking.
Collect samples of the children's work. Develop a procedure for judging what kinds of work would be expected in the more open classroom.
Select a group of children and follow them intensively for several days to see what activities they pursue and how their activities are decided.

THE OBSERVATION RECORD

Our next task was to develop an instrument to measure motivation. The observation record, an instrument that the instructor had used in prior research, appeared appropriate, given our limited time for instrument development. The observation record procedure is as follows: During each of six, consecutive, five-minute intervals, the classroom observer records the number of students who are judged *not* to be attending to any learning activity for at least one-half the time (defined as two and a half minutes). Attending to a learning activity is defined as having one's sensory apparatus directed toward some object(s) that contains academic content (broadly defined). Thus nonattenders are primarily those who have materials such as books open, but are not looking at them, and those who are engaged in social conversation or routine preparatory activities such as pencil sharpening. The number of nonattenders is divided by the total number of students to give the percent of nonattenders. The score is obtained by averaging across the six intervals.

Briefly describe at least one procedure that you could use to determine the reliability of the observation record:

_____

_____

_____

_____

Next, describe at least one procedure that you would recommend for obtaining empirical evidence of the validity of the observation record:

_____

_____

_____

_____

This is an appropriate time for you to use the two instruments: the rating scale and the observation record. Locate some kind of classroom situation, not necessarily with children nor exemplifying the open classroom. The instruments can be used in any classroom setting. Spend at least ten minutes observing the classroom; then rate it on the fourteen items of the rating scale (table 2.2). At another time, take at least one five-minute observation period and apply the procedure for assessing motivation on the observation record. It will be of more value if you can do more than one five-minute observation.

Record your evaluation of the two instruments based on your tryout. Pay particular attention to validity, that is, the extent to which the instruments seem to provide a measurement of the attributes that they are intended to measure. Give reasons for your opinions.

Your evaluation of the logical validity of the rating scale:

_____

_____

_____

_____

_____

_____

_____

_____

_____

Your evaluation of the logical validity of the observation record: _____

_____

_____

_____

_____

_____

_____

_____

_____

_____

AUTHOR'S COMMENTS

The rating scale was used by several pairs of observers working independently in the same classroom at the same time. In spite of only limited training in the use of the scale being given, most pairs of observers agreed quite well in their ratings.[3] Subsequent discussion suggested that certain items were difficult to rate, particularly those dealing with how the teacher is addressed (item 11), use of resource people (item 4), and furniture arrangement (item 5). Consequently, the validity of these items is questionable.

In spite of the obvious difficulties in observing whether another person is paying attention or not, the observation record does provide a reliable and useful measurement of classroom attention when used by observers who have received prior training in its administration and when several visits are made to each classroom and the average used as the measurement. Its validity rests on the assumption that a group that appears to be attending closely is in fact attending closely. This instrument provides an index of only one limited aspect of what is encompassed by the term motivation. Consequently, the scale ultimately must be judged of questionable validity for the purpose of the open classroom study. At this point, had our purpose been sophisticated research rather than instruction, we would have had to either locate or develop additional instruments or revise our hypothesis to specify attention rather than motivation.

Instruments differ as to the amount of training required in their use. In general, observation techniques require considerable training for optimal use. Training usually consists of explanation and discussion of procedures, followed by use of the procedures by trainees in a standard situation such as video-taped or live classroom where all observe the same behaviors, followed by discussion of differences. This process, or variations thereon, is repeated until an acceptable level of agreement of independent observers is reached.

In the preceding pages you have seen examples of two common forms of instrumentation: the rating scale and the observation record. In the succeeding pages there are examples of other widely used forms of instrumentation.

---

[3]In chapter five, techniques for giving numerical substance to such terms as *quite well* will be discussed.

THE STRUCTURED INTERVIEW

The *structured interview* is an instrument by which individuals are asked to respond to a series of specific questions. An example of this instrument was developed when another of the author's classes expressed interest in the open classroom. The study focused on assessing student opinion on a variety of issues that were of theoretical interest as well as of interest to the teachers in a particular school. The instrument developed was used to interview a sample of children from each of ten classrooms in a new school that had from its beginning used the open classroom approach. The structured interview technique requires that the interviewers follow the precise wording of the questions. However, they may be allowed some latitude in the clarification of terms. It is important, of course, that the interviewer do nothing to bias or influence the answers being given. It is equally important that the interviewer establish a degree of rapport with the child before beginning to ask the questions. The questions, shown in table 2.3, were intended for use with children in grades four through six.

Locate a student in grades four through six and conduct the interview with him. Some questions may be inappropriate, and you may delete them. However, it is important that you use as many as possible. Record the student responses. After completing the interview, record your reactions to the questions with particular emphasis on their validity. Are you clear about what each question is intended to measure? Do you think your student understood all the questions? Do you think he was giving you his real opinions on all questions? What is your evaluation of the overall validity of this particular structured interview as you understand its purpose?

TABLE 2.3
INTERVIEW SCHEDULE

Questions	Student Responses
1 a. How do you feel[4] about your teacher?	_____
b. Why?	_____
c. How do the other kids in the class feel about the teacher?	_____
2 a. Do most of the kids in the room like their class-mates?	_____
b. How does it compare to last year?	_____
c. How do you feel about having different ages in the same class?	_____
d. Is there much fighting?	_____
e. How does it compare to last year?	_____
f. How do you settle problems?	_____
3 a. Do most of the kids in the class find school interesting?	_____
b. Why?	_____
c. If you couldn't come to school for some reason, would you be disappointed?	_____

[4]As was discussed in chapter one, terms such as *feel* are ambiguous and need to be clarified in the researcher's mind. This does not preclude their use in instruments where their ambiguity may, in fact, be an asset when one does not wish to limit responses too narrowly.

Questions	Student Responses
4 a. Are you doing more kinds of things this year than last?	_____
b. What things?	_____
c. Do you do a lot of things without being told to do them?	_____
d. More than last year?	_____
e. How do you feel about doing more things?	_____
5 a. Is this classroom a happy place for you?	_____
b. How does it compare to last year?	_____
6 a. How do you feel about the amount of noise in the room?	_____
b. How does it compare to last year?	_____
7 a. Do you help your classmates with their work when they ask you?	_____
b. Do you ask other kids for help with things you do not understand?	_____
8 a. Are the things you are learning in school important to you?	_____
b. How does it compare with last year?	_____
9 a. Do you talk with your parents about what you do in school?	_____

Questions	Student Responses

b.   How much?

_____

c.   What do they say about
it?

_____

d.   Do your parents say any
bad things about school?

_____

    Evaluation of the logical validity of this structured

interview: _____

_____

_____

_____

_____

_____

AUTHOR'S COMMENTS

Our use of the structured interview consisted of individual interviews with six children selected as representative of each of ten classrooms. The children in each class were in grades four through six, represented a variety of ethnic groups, and, for the most part, represented the lower socioeconomic level. Most of the questions were understandable to the children and appeared to function as had been intended. The exceptions were the four questions that asked about talking with their parents about school. These were somewhat unclear to some of the students.

There was considerable difference among the ten classrooms on certain questions. For example, in one classroom all six of the children said "yes," the things they were learning in school were important to them; in another classroom, only two of the six answered "yes." A question of validity was raised, however, by the finding that in the first of these classrooms, only one of the six children said that it was better than last year, whereas in the second all six said it was better than last year. This inconsistency raised some questions about the validity of either or both questions. Further, since it was not feasible to take the time to train our interviewers in this situation, it is conceivable that differences among interviewers in the style of interviewing or the way in which the questions were asked may have influenced children's responses.

On logical grounds one might question the interview procedure because the interviewer was not known to the children. Further, the interviews, as we conducted them, were done in the class setting and one might expect a reluctance on the part of elementary age children to make negative statements about their teacher or their school even if they were felt.

As a part of the same study we also observed in these classrooms and rated them on the same characteristics as those sampled in the children's questions. We discovered a considerable correspondence between the assessment of a particular classroom based on what the children said and the impressions gained from observation. This is some evidence that both procedures are to some extent valid (recall page 45).

In summary, I think that this measure leaves a good deal to be desired. It would certainly need to be further refined before being widely used. However, there is some evidence, primarily in terms of its agreement with observations, that even as it is presently constituted, it has some degree of validity.

Since interviewing is time consuming, questions such as these are often printed and distributed as questionnaires. This procedure has as a major drawback the likelihood that a substantial number will not be returned unless they are filled out in a group setting, which may itself influence responses.

The following suggestions should be helpful in preparing questions for either interviews or questionnaires.[5]

1. Keep the purpose of the study in mind as you prepare each question.

2. Word questions to keep the respondent attentive.

3. Avoid complex and/or ambiguous words or phrasing.

4. Keep in mind the probable frame of reference of the respondent.

5. Avoid unrealistic assumptions about the respondent's level of background information.

6. Avoid leading questions, i.e., questions that suggest an expected or right answer.

7. Give the questions a sensible sequence from the respondent's point of view.

8. Place general questions before specific ones.

9. Place questions that may be offensive to the respondent toward the end.

10. Do not let one question (or its response) influence answers to subsequent questions.

ABILITY TESTS

If you have lived in our society for any appreciable length of time, you are quite familiar with ability tests. The most common ability tests are the so-called achievement tests that range from kindergarten (e.g., Metropolitan Reading Readiness)[6] through graduate school (e.g., Graduate Record Examination). Another type is the so-called intelligence test, which assesses intellectual abilities that are less directly related to what is taught in school. The vast literature on this type of instrument (and on some particular tests) demonstrates that many of these tests are very reliable and valid when used with some

---

[5]Adapted from Cannel, C. and Kahn, R., "The Collection of Data by Interviewing" in *Research Methods in the Behavioral Sciences*, Festinger, L. and Katz, D., eds. (New York, N.Y.: Dryden, 1953), pp. 327-380; and from Phillips, B., *Social Research, Strategy and Tactics* (New York, N.Y.: MacMillan, 1966), p. 120.

[6]Unless otherwise referenced, all specific tests mentioned in this chapter are discussed in Anastasi, A., *Psychological Testing* (New York, N.Y.: MacMillan, 1954).

persons and for certain purposes (for example, predicting college grades of middle-class Caucasians). At the same time, they are increasingly under attack when used with other persons and/or for other purposes, such as identifying Mexican-Americans for special classes. Further, there is increasing recognition that many important abilities exist that these tests do not measure (such as the ability to see unusual relationships). Consequently, a researcher must carefully evaluate any such test before using it and judge whether it is appropriate to the purpose of his study. In doing so, logical validity plays an important role. In addition, however, one should look for empirical evidence (in test manuals, research reports, or test reviews) of reliability and validity. A numerical index that is useful in this regard (the correlation coefficient) is discussed in chapter five. Table 2.4 is a nontypical intelligence test; please take it. Answer each of the questions in the space provided.

TABLE 2.4
THE Q-E INTELLIGENCE TEST

Directions: Please allow no more than ten minutes to take this
test. Answer all questions in the space provided.

_____ 1. I went to bed at eight o'clock in the evening and
set the alarm to get up at nine in the morning.
How many hours of sleep would this allow me?

_____ 2. Who invented the Bunsen Burner?

_____ 3. Some months have thirty days, some have thirty-one;
how many have twenty-eight days?

_____ 4. If you had only one match and entered a dark room
where there was an oil lamp, oil heater, and some
kindling wood, which would you light first?

_____ 5. If a doctor gave you three pills and told you to
take one every half hour, how long would they last?

_____ 6. A man builds a house with four sides to it, a rec-
tangular structure, each having a southern exposure.
A big bear comes wandering by. What color is the
bear?

_____ 7. A farmer had seventeen sheep. All but nine died.
How many did he have left?

_____ 8. Divide 30 by 1/2. Add 10. What is the answer?

_____ 9. Take two apples from three apples. What do you
have?

_____10. How many animals of each species did Moses take
aboard the Ark?

Now look at the answer key on page 62 and score yourself.
Give yourself one point for each correct answer. This test can
be used to illustrate a way of assessing reliability. Presumably the score on this test gives a measure of intelligence. If
so, each of the ten items should be an indicator of intelligence.
We could then use only five items instead of ten. Suppose we
used items 1, 3, 5, 7, and 9 as our test. What would your score
be? We could just as well use items 2, 4, 6, 8, and 10. What
would your score be on those five items? Compare the two scores.
If either half of the test provides an equally good measurement

of intelligence, your scores should agree fairly well. If they
don't, then the two five-item tests do not give consistent results. If this is true, then the total test (ten items) probably does not give consistent results either, in which case the
test would not be considered reliable.

Ask some other people to take the test. Give them each a
score on each of the separate five-item tests.

Person	Score on Five-item test #1 Items 1, 3, 5, 7, 9	Score on Five-item test #2 Items 2, 4, 6, 8, 10
You	_____	_____
#1	_____	_____
#2	_____	_____
#3	_____	_____
#4	_____	_____
#5	_____	_____

Examine these results. What do you conclude (based on this
small amount of evidence) about the reliability of this test?

_____

_____

_____

_____

Key to Q-E Intelligence Test

1.	One hour	6.	White
2.	Bunsen	7.	Nine
3.	All of them	8.	70
4.	Match	9.	Two
5.	One hour	10.	None (wrong captain)

AUTHOR'S COMMENTS

If the two scores for each person are identical, this suggests that the test is highly reliable. If, on the other hand, many people have discrepancies of 3, 4, or 5 points, this suggests very low reliability. Results obtained by my research students indicate that the test has fair reliability but not good enough for drawing conclusions about individuals. (Most scores differed by 1 or 2 points, but a sizeable number differed by 3 or more points.)

We have examined only one aspect of reliability for this test. We still do not know how much a person's score might change from one time to another. We could get a better idea if we gave one of the five-item tests at one time and the other five-item test at another. If feasible, you might want to try doing so with some individuals and making a table like the one above. These procedures are the ones actually followed in most attempts to assess test reliability. To do it properly, one should use more people (at least one hundred or so). Most tests contain many more than ten items because it has been found that tests with more items are usually more reliable, presumably because they provide a larger sampling of a person's behavior.

What is your analysis of the logical validity of the Q-E Intelligence Test? Do you think it measures intelligence? Why or why not?

_____

_____

_____

_____

AUTHOR'S COMMENTS

*This test appears to measure primarily one's lack of gulli-
bility or one's ability to see through attempts to mislead.
Whether this is intelligence depends on one's definition or view
of intelligence. It would seem that most current psychological
definitions would incorporate lack of gullibility as one, but
only one, of many aspects of intelligence. The test also appears to measure knowledge to some extent. It would be expected
that almost anyone in our society over the age of ten would understand the concept of time as it appears in item 1. In contrast, one must have at least a passing acquaintance with the
Judeo-Christian tradition in order for item 10 to function as an
indicator of gullibility. Also, item 8 clearly requires knowledge of dividing by fractions. The entire test assumes sufficient ability to read English to comprehend the statements; some
recent immigrants would receive a low score on this basis alone.
Adquate evaluation of the validity of this test would depend on
research that explores the relationship of this test to other
measures. This test is an adaptation of a teaching "test" widely used in tests and measurement courses; the original author is
unknown.*

Existing tests are frequently criticized because they do
not adequately measure "higher cognitive skills" or "thinking
skills" such as making legitimate inferences from information,
recognizing assumptions, making logically defensible deductions,
and applying ideas to new contexts. *The Watson-Glaser Critical
Thinking Appraisal* is a published test that attempts to measure
some of these characteristics in people of high school age or
over. A description of other similar instruments developed as
part of the classic "Eight Year Study" can be found in *Appraising and Recording Student Progress.*[7]

A more recent test, *The Application of Generalizations
Test*, was developed by the author in conjunction with *The Taba
Curriculum Development Project in Social Studies.*[8] This test
assesses the ability to apply previously learned ideas to a new
context. One of the objectives of the Taba Curriculum is that
children will, through inductive processes, learn important
ideas or generalizations in social studies and will subsequently
apply these generalizations in new contexts. The test, designed
specifically for sixth graders, consists of seven passages, each

---

[7]Smith, E. R. and others, *Appraising and Recording Student Progress* (New York, N.Y.: Harper, 1942).

[8]Wallen, N., Durkin, M., Fraenkel, J., McNaughton, A., and Sawin,
E., *The Taba Curriculum Development Project in Social Studies*,
U.S.O.E. #6-10-182 (Menlo Park, Calif.: Addison-Wesley, 1969).

followed by a series of statements. There are a total of sixty-five statements. Both the passages and the statements are read to the student group so as not to penalize poor readers. The student is asked to respond to each statement as "probably true" or "probably false," having been made aware in the directions that a clear true or false answer is, in most cases, not defensible. The example shown in table 2.5 includes one passage and the statements to which the student responds. Also shown are the generalizations that are intended to be applied to each item. These do not appear on the test as administered. The student follows along as the passage and statements are read. After the examiner reads each statement, the student marks his answer. The statements cannot be answered from the text alone; the student must use other ideas (or guess). The student who has learned the ideas intended by the curriculum will supposedly be able to apply them to the situation and respond to the statements. For example, the student who has grasped the generalization listed next to statement 1 should answer "probably true."

TABLE 2.5
EXAMPLE FROM APPLICATION OF GENERALIZATIONS TEST

Hunteros and Farmanos

This is about two groups of people, the Hunteros and Farmanos, who live in the same valley surrounded by mountains. The Hunteros hunt and fish to get food. They often have to move because the herds of animals move from place to place. Most of the Farmanos are farmers. However, some of them make simple tools.

Remember: Hunteros are hunters
Farmanos are farmers

Statements	Generalizations (Not included in test as administered.)
(PT)* 1. The Farmanos have more schools for their children than the Hunteros.	1. Geographic stability and increased technology lead to more formalized educational institutions, permanent buildings, etc.
(PF)* 2. The Hunteros' way of life shows that their ability to learn is less than the Farmanos.	2. "Way of life" is not a good index of learning ability; it is a product of many factors.

*(PT): Probably True; (PF): Probably False

	Statements		Generalizations
(PT)	3.	The Farmanos should be worried if the Hunteros have a poor hunting season.	3. Interdependence of groups in same geographic area is likely. If one group suffers, it has repercussions on others.
(PT)	4.	The Farmanos will develop modern conveniences before the Hunteros.	4. Technology breeds technology.
(PF)	5.	The Hunteros have practically no contacts with the Farmanos.	5. Groups living in the same geographic area almost certainly interact.
(PT)	6.	The Farmanos are suspicious of the Hunteros.	6. Strangeness or differences among groups usually lead to distrust or suspicion.
(PT)	7.	The Hunteros will be more concerned that their leaders be daring than will the Farmanos.	7. Expectations for leaders depend largely on group needs.
(PF)	8.	The Hunteros do not have musical or artistic activities.	8. Almost all cultures or societies have some forms of art.
(PT)	9.	The Farmanos will increase in number (population) faster than the Hunteros.	9. Geographic stability and a less hazardous life lead to population growth.
(PT)	10.	If both groups had their lodgings destroyed, this would harm the Farmanos more than the Hunteros.	10. Geographic stability leads to greater investment, economically and psychologically, in permanent structures.

Indicate your overall impression of the validity of these particular statements for measuring the student's ability to apply specified generalizations. Also list any statements that seem to have questionable validity and your reasons.

Evaluation of logical validity for Application of Generalizations Test (overall evaluation): _____

_____

_____

_____

_____

Specific Statements of Questionable Validity	Reasons
_____	_____
_____	_____
_____	_____
_____	_____
_____	_____
_____	_____

AUTHOR'S COMMENTS

The main validity information available on this test was obtained by giving the test in an interview format with a sampling of thirty-one sixth-grade students. Both the passage and questions were read to the students as they followed along with their own copies. The students were to answer probably true or probably false and to explain their answers. The task of the interviewer was to pursue the point until the rationale and thought process that had led to the answer was made clear. These interviews were recorded verbatim and subsequently typescripted, making it possible for them to be reviewed independently by two analysts. Each response to a statement by a student was classified in one of fifteen different categories that covered all possible responses. Only the five major categories are presented here. Each of the categories is illustrated using an early version of statement 2: "The Hunteros live the way they do because they are less able to learn than the Farmanos." Responses such as the one in category 5, which suggested that some students interpreted the question as school learning, led to the revised wording that appears in the final form.

TABLE 2.6
EXAMPLES OF CATEGORIES FOR INTERVIEW STUDY
OF APPLICATION OF GENERALIZATIONS TEST

Category 1: Answered correctly, using intended generalization (regardless of particular wording).
> Example: "Not necessarily, because instead of learning to . . . , that's their way of life. They learned how to hunt and the others learned how to farm, so it's probably false."

Category 2: Answered correctly, using different but defensible generalization or rationale.
> Example: "Well, I think that's false because they move around a lot, and, well, they can learn things."

Category 3: Answered correctly, based on erroneous generalization or reasoning.
> Example: "Well, I think that's probably false because neither one of them has schools."

Category 4: Answered incorrectly, using erroneous generalizations or reasons.
> Example: "True, because they have the tools to do all of their fishing and hunting and cooking and stuff."

Category 5: Answered incorrectly, using a defensible generalization or reason.
> Example: "I think it's true because the Farmanos can build
> schools. They can go to them and learn all the knowledge.
> The Hunteros keep on moving around and they don't have a
> school to learn."

*Responses in categories 1, 2, and 4 indicate that the
statement is functioning as intended. That is, the students who
get it right are using an appropriate generalization and logical
reasoning. The students getting the wrong answer are doing so
because they used an erroneous idea or illogical reasoning.
Categories 3 and 5, however, indicate that the question is not
functioning properly. For example, in category 3 the student
gave the right answer, as keyed, but based it on an erroneous
idea; in category 5, the student gave the wrong answer, although
his ideas and thought processes are appropriate and logical.*

*This analysis was carried out for all of the sixty-five
statements in the test. It was done independently by two analysts. At the conclusion of this analysis, the categorization
of student responses made by the two analysts agreed quite well.
A score was derived on the basis of the student's reasoning
process as revealed in the interview. An answer in categories
1, 2, or 5 was considered correct. This score agreed quite well
with the score obtained from the student's initial answer of
"probably true" or "probably false." This analysis showed that,
in general, the test was functioning as it was intended. There
were, however, certain statements that were identified by this
analysis as poor statements. These were deleted or altered.*

*A better way to assess the test's validity would be to use
other instruments such as teacher ratings to see if students
scoring high on the test were also identified as high in ability
to apply the specified ideas.*

How might an instrument of this type be used in the open

classroom study and why would it be valuable? _____

_____

_____

_____

_____

AUTHOR'S COMMENTS

An ability test is sometimes used as a measure of motiva-
tion. The task must be such that one's score reflects not
ability but persistence or motivation. Whether such a test
could be designed to fit the definition of motivation used is
problematical. It is difficult to see how one could use an
ability test to measure openness.

PROJECTIVE TESTS

Projective tests have a unique feature; they permit the individual to project himself into the test. This type of test
has no clear-cut right answers, and the format of the test permits the individual to express something of his own personality,
with room for a wide variety of possible responses. The best
known examples of this approach are the Rorschach Ink Blot Test,[9]
in which an individual is asked to tell what the blots look like
to him; and the Thematic Apperception Test (TAT), in which pictures of events are presented and the individual is asked to
make up a story about them. Another format is the cartoon approach, the best known example of which is the Rosensweig Picture Frustration Study. An application of this approach to the
classroom setting is the Picture Situation Inventory.[10] This
test consists of a series of cartoon-like drawings, each portraying a classroom situation. Each situation depicts a child
saying something and the person taking the test is to enter the
response of the teacher, thereby presumably indicating something
of his own tendencies in such a situation. Two of the pictures
are reproduced in figure 2.1. Fill in your own reactions in the
balloons. In doing so, place yourself in the position of the
teacher in the cartoon.

---

[9] See note 4.

[10] Rowan, N. T., *The Relationship of Teacher Interaction in
Classroom Situations to Teacher Personality Variables* (Un-
published doctoral dissertation, University of Utah, 1967).
Used by permission.

FIGURE 2.1
SAMPLE ITEMS FROM PICTURE SITUATION INVENTORY

With tests of this kind, or with any open-ended procedure
that permits a wide variety of possible responses, some procedure must be developed for arriving at a score. One technique,
a variety of content analysis, is to define categories, based
on a sample of responses. Once developed, new responses can be
categorized by comparing them with examples of each category.
This procedure was illustrated previously (table 2.6) in connec-
tion with the Application of Generalization Test. For the Picture Situation Inventory, scoring systems have been developed to
assess two characteristics of teachers. These are control need,
defined as the extent to which a teacher is motivated to control
the moment to moment activities of her students; and communication, defined as the extent to which the teacher attempts to
keep channels of communication open. The scoring system permits
assignment of 1 to 5 points on each picture for each characteristic. Each point-category is described and several examples
given. Abbreviated examples of the scoring categories for the
two pictures are given in table 2.7. Two examples of each
point-category are shown.

TABLE 2.7
SCORING CATEGORIES FOR THE PICTURE SITUATION INVENTORY

Control Need Score: Rationale, the more controlling or directive the response, the higher the score.

Picture 1: 1 point, "I thought you would enjoy something special."
"Is this a job you should do?"

2 points, "I'd like to see how well you can do it."
"Would you like me to help?"

3 points, "Some children don't do as well or as much as others."
"You and Tom are two different children."

4 points, "Yes, I would appreciate it if you would finish it."
"Yes, sometimes children do different things."

5 points, "This is your assignment, not Tom's."
"Do it quickly, please."

Picture 2: 1 point, "Do you think you would like a harder book?"
"Do you want to?"

2 points, "All right, why don't you try this one."
"Why don't I discuss it with your mother."

3 points, "Let's hear you read and then I'll decide where you should be reading."
"If you'll read two easier ones while I help you with the harder ones, maybe we can keep everybody happy."

4 points, "For now, let's read where we are comfortable. Before long we can read harder books."
"I will call your mother and talk to her so she'll understand why you are in that book."

5 points, "When we are able, we'll read in a hard book."
"Tell mother we have a regular method of progressing from one book to another. When this one is completed, we'll go to another."

Communication Score: Rationale, the more the response keeps communication open, the higher the score.

Picture 1: 1 point,   "Yes, please do as you were told."
                      "This is your assignment, not Tom's."

           2 points, "I have reasons for wanting you to do it."
                      "Yes, Tom doesn't need the practice."

           3 points, "You do things for your own benefit."
                      "You and Tom are two different children."

           4 points, "I thought you would enjoy something special."
                      "I'd like to see how well you can do it."

           5 points, "Would you like me to help?"
                      "Why don't you want to do it?"

Picture 2: 1 point,   "Tell your mother we have a regular system
                      for progressing.
                      "Why doesn't your mother talk to me about
                      such things?"

           2 points, "I'll call your mother and explain why
                      you're in this book."
                      "I don't think you're ready yet."

           3 points, "You can when you are able to."
                      "Let's hear you read and then I'll decide
                      where you should be reading."

           4 points, "Do you think you can?"
                      "Why don't I discuss it with your mother?"

           5 points, "Do you want to?"
                      "Let's see if we can find one you'll like."

Score your own responses using the scoring categories in table 2.7. First, compare your response to picture 1 to the examples listed under "Control Need Score—Picture 1." Find the example closest to your own (keeping in mind the characteristic being assessed) and enter the point score below. Then compare the same response (yours) to those listed under "Communication—Picture 1" in the same way and enter it. Repeat the procedure for Picture 2.

	Control	Communication
Picture 1	_____	_____
Picture 2	_____	_____
Total	_____	_____

How well do the two scores for each characteristic agree?
Next add the two scores for control together and do the same for
communication. How well do these scores correspond to your view
of your own probable (or actual) behavior in the classroom? Do
they agree with your perception of your need to control or with
the extent to which you keep communication with students open?
Based on this analysis, write your evaluation of the validity of
the two projective pictures.

Evaluation of validity for Picture Situation Inventory,

picture 1, Control Need: _____

_____

_____

_____

Communication: _____

_____

_____

_____

Evaluation of validity for Picture Situation Inventory,

picture 2, Control Need: _____

_____

_____

_____

_____

Communication: _____

_____

_____

_____

_____

AUTHOR'S COMMENTS

In addition to the appeal to logical or apparent validity, there is some evidence in support of the validity of these two measures (control and communication) when they are based on all of the twenty pictures in the total test. It is summarized below.

Rowan[11] studied relationships between the two Picture Situation Inventory (PSI) scores and several other measures with a group of elementary school teachers. She found that teachers scoring high on control need were more likely to: (a) be seen by classroom observers as imposing themselves on situations and having a higher content emphasis; (b) be judged by interviewers as having more rigid attitudes of right and wrong, less acceptance of themselves, and lower feelings of self-worth; and (c) score higher on a test of authoritarian tendencies. Teachers scoring high on communication were more likely to: (a) be observed as doing less imposing; (b) be judged by interviewers as having less rigid attitudes of right and wrong, more acceptance of themselves, and higher feeling of self-worth; and (c) be judged better teachers by administrators.

In a study of ability to predict success in a program preparing teachers for inner-city classrooms, the author found evidence that the PSI control score had predictive value. Although the study had serious limitations, there were relationships between the control score obtained on entrance to the program and a variety of measures subsequently obtained through classroom observation in the student teaching and subsequent first-year teaching assignments. The most clear-cut finding was that the persons scoring higher in control need had classrooms observed as less noisy. This finding adds somewhat to the validity of this measurement since one would expect the teacher with higher control need to have a quieter room.

The reliability of both measures was found to be high when assessed by the procedure used on page 62. When assessed by a follow-up over a period of eight years, the consistency was considerably lower, as would be expected.[12]

---

[11]Rowan, N. T., *The Relationship of Teacher Interaction in Classroom Situations to Teacher Personality Variables* (Unpublished doctoral dissertation, University of Utah, 1967).

[12]*Sausalito Teacher Education Project, Annual Reports 1968, 1969, 1970* (San Francisco State College, Calif.).

79   Projective Tests

How might a projective test be used in the open classroom
study? _____

_____

_____

_____

_____

AUTHOR'S COMMENTS

One might portray classroom situations of various kinds such as students doing a variety of things or student conflict. Then have students and/or teachers write in responses of individuals as in the PSI. A measure of openness might be obtainable from the responses. With respect to motivation, a considerable literature exists on the use of the TAT (page 72) and similar instruments for assessing certain motivations (e.g., achievement, affiliation, power) in adults.[13] Adaptations might be appropriate for this study.

You have now seen examples of the most commonly used forms of instrumentation. They constitute only an introduction to the topic. There are a number of excellent references that expand upon this topic in detail. Some of them are listed at the end of this chapter.

The next task is for you to determine the instrumentation for the study that you are planning. You have essentially two choices: either locate an existing instrument(s) that could be used in your study or develop your own instrument. For purposes of an introductory course, it is probably appropriate to attempt to develop your own instrument, provided it is in the form of a rating scale, a structured interview, a questionnaire, or an observational record. It is unlikely that you will have sufficient time to develop the other forms of instrumentation that have been discussed here.

Write down the proposed means of instrumentation for your study. If you plan to use instruments that you have located, identify them by name and description. If appropriate, include sample items, and then write an analysis of the appropriateness of this instrument for your purpose. If you plan to develop your own instrument, describe the procedure that you will follow and include at least some sample items or some examples from the instrument itself.

It may not be appropriate for you to spend a great deal of time developing your own instrument. However, it is necessary that you use some form of instrumentation in the information gathering aspect of your study. You will probably want to return to this section and add to it as time goes on. At this point, record as much as possible regarding the instrument you are planning to use or develop. As soon as you have your instrumentation firmed up, ask another person(s), preferably one

---

[13]See, for example, Atkinson, J. W., ed., *Motives in Fantasy, Action and Society* (New York, N.Y.: D. Van Nostrand, 1958).

knowledgeable about research, to assess the logical validity of
your instrument(s). Ask whether they think the instrument(s)
will measure what you are after and record their response. To
the extent possible, try out your instrument. There is no sub-
stitute for tryout and concomitant evaluation.

Instrumentation for your study: _____

_____

_____

_____

_____

_____

_____

_____

_____

_____

_____

_____

_____

Evaluation of validity by another person: _____

_____

_____

_____

_____

_____

_____

How could you assess the reliability of your instrument(s)?

_____

_____

How could you collect empirical evidence on the validity of your instrument(s) for your purpose? _____

_____

_____

SUMMARY

You have become acquainted with some of the major types of instruments and have examined a few in some detail. You also have available some criteria for use in evaluating an instrument. You have at least begun to select or develop instruments for your own study. This process of instrumentation will probably need to be continued as we move ahead to other topics. We are now ready for the next topic, which is sampling or the obtaining of subjects.

Major concepts considered in this chapter were:

Instrument	Ability Test
Measurement	Projective Test
Rating Scale	Reliability
Observation Record	Logical Validity
Structured Interview	Empirical Validity

REFERENCES FOR FURTHER READING

Anastasi, A. *Psychological Testing*. New York, N.Y.: MacMillan, 1956.

Bloom, B. S., ed. *Taxonomy of Educational Objectives, Handbook I: Cognitive Domain*. New York, N.Y.: David McKay, 1956.

Cronbach, L. J. *Essentials of Psychological Testing*. 2d ed. New York, N.Y.: Harper & Row, 1960.

Krathwahl, D. R., Bloom, B. S., and Masia, B. B. *Taxonomy of Educational Objectives, Handbook II: Affective Domain.* New York, N.Y.: David McKay, 1964.

Levine, S. and Elzey, F. *A Programmed Introduction to Educational and Psychological Measurement.* Monterey, Calif.: Brooks/Cole, 1970.

Sawin, E. *Evaluation and the Work of the Teacher.* Belmont, Calif.: Wadsworth, 1969.

Wood, D. A. *Test Construction.* Columbus, Ohio: Charles Merrill, 1961.

In addition to these books, you should be aware of a publication entitled, *The Mental Measurements Yearbook* by O. K. Buros (Gryphon Press). This publication appears every few years and is a systematic review and critique of all commercially published tests. Another source of information about tests is test publisher's catalogs. Some of the major publishers of tests are Educational Testing Service (ETS), The Psychological Corporation, and The California Test Bureau.

In addition, there are many instruments that are developed for particular purposes, such as research studies, which are not published commercially and which are not at the present time systematically cataloged. These are best identified by reading the literature pertinent to the research problem.

3

Sampling
or "Where Do the Findings Apply?"

INTRODUCTION

A major consideration in any study is the sample, i.e., the individuals or groups on which information is to be obtained. Who is to be observed, questioned, tested? After completing this chapter you should be able to recognize examples of poor sampling and/or inappropriate generalizing of results. You will have identified both an ideal and a feasible procedure for selecting subjects for your proposed study.

Once again the open classroom study provides an illustration. After some discussion about how data might be collected to test the hypothesis, "The more open the classroom, the higher the motivation of the students," the research class decided to try to identify classrooms that would show differences with regard to openness and then find out how they compared with regard to student motivation. The class decided to study only the elementary school level: (a) because the class contained mostly elementary level school personnel; and (b) in order to delimit the study. There were a number of elementary schools in the local area that, by reputation, represented more openness than others. By contacting these schools, we determined that it would be possible for members of the class to visit these schools.

The next question was how many classrooms to study. The sample that was decided upon consisted of twenty-seven classrooms in five schools. This number—twenty-seven—evolved from considerations of desirability and feasibility. For reasons discussed later, it is almost always desirable to have as large a sample as is feasible. It was considered, however, that for this study a sample of twenty-seven classrooms was adequate, although not as large as was desired. There are no clear-cut rules for deciding on sample size. If a good deal is known about the measuring instruments and about the subjects, it is possible to employ a rather technical procedure to estimate the sample size necessary to provide a good test of the hypothesis. However, in many studies this degree of detailed information does not exist. A rule of thumb: it is desirable to have a sample of at least thirty; however, a larger sample is all to the good and should be used whenever possible. Note that the sample size involves the units that are measured. In many studies the units are individual people. In the open classroom study, however, the hypothesis deals with classrooms; hence the classroom, not the individual student, is the unit of sampling and measurement.

After the five schools had been identified and permission given to collect the kind of information that we desired, forty classrooms in grades four through six were made available to us. These grades became the focus of our study because we were concerned that the primary grades might pose difficulty in using our instruments (you may recall we originally wished to interview students). We settled upon twenty-seven classrooms because we had a total of eighteen people to be involved in the data collection and wished to have two individuals collecting data at the same time in each classroom so that we could compare their measurements. This meant that we would have nine teams of two people each. The time available to us for data collection was one afternoon and it seemed feasible for each team to visit three classrooms, giving us a total number of twenty-seven. In this way we solved the issue of feasibility. The actual sample on which data were collected was twenty-six classrooms since one team of observers was able to visit only two rather than three classrooms.

If one is to do educational research—particularly in schools—one must come to grips with such practical questions as: Can we get permission to visit the classrooms? Will the school staff be cooperative? How much data can we collect given our human and financial resources? If one is not prepared to consider such feasibility questions, he had better return to the laboratory.

In planning a study one will not expect to encounter such severe and artificial restrictions as inevitably accompany a class project. Nevertheless, the type of planning presented above must be done in any study. In some cases, feasibility restrictions may be so severe as to result in the judgment that the likelihood of an adequate test of the hypothesis is too slight to undertake data collection.

It is important in any study to describe the sample and how it was obtained in as much detail as possible. In this study the team of observers assigned to each school asked the principal to identify classrooms that represented the open classroom style. They made an effort to observe in at least one or two of these classrooms as well as in one or two classrooms not so identified, if such classrooms were to be found in the school. Aside from this, the observers simply chose classrooms to visit with no particular system in mind. In order to include one of the five schools, second and third grades were observed. Therefore, the final sample, although drawn predominantly from intermediate grades, included several primary classrooms.

GENERALIZING

At this point it is necessary to introduce an extremely important idea: *generalizing* from a particular study. We generalize whenever we apply the findings of a study to people or settings other than the *particular* people and setting used in obtaining data for the study. In the case of the open classroom study, we are generalizing if we in any way state or imply that our findings would apply to any classrooms other than the ones we studied. Science is built upon the idea of generalizing. Every science seeks to find basic laws that can be applied in a great many situations and, in the case of the social sciences, generalized to many people. In so-called applied research one also may wish to generalize. For example, if research suggests that a particular teaching method or set of materials is effective in a particular school, one may want to apply that method to other settings with other people. The only time one is *not* interested in generalizing is when the results of an investigation are of interest only as applied to a particular group of people at a particular time and where all of the members of the group are included in the sample.

We are often guilty of generalizing without being aware that we are doing so, as when the results of a study are publicized with a disclaimer that the investigator was interested only in the subjects of that study. If this were true, what would be the justification for publishing the results? If the results have no generalizability to other situations or persons, how could the reader be expected to find any utility for them?

Can you specify some situations in which a study would have value if applied only to the particular subjects used in the sample? One example might be a study of the opinions of a school faculty on a particular issue such as a program of ethnic studies. It might be of value for decision making or program planning to know the opinions of specified groups of people at a particular time without generalizing to other groups or other settings. Even here, however, one must be aware of the temptation to generalize any findings to other faculties in other settings.

Examples of studies where generalizing would *not* be in-

tended: 1._____

_____

_____

_____

2. _____

_____

_____

_____

     If, as is more common, we are really interested in general-
izing our findings, two criteria must be satisfied. First, en-
vironmental conditions must be the same in all important respects in any new situation to which one wishes to generalize
(e.g., physical plant, community attitudes). This point will be
considered in more detail in chapter four. Here we are concerned with the second criterion: the subjects in a study must
be representative of the larger group to which one wishes to
generalize. The *sample* in a study is the actual units of study
(usually people) on whom data is collected. The *population* in
a study is any group (with a certain set of identifiable characteristics) to which one wishes to generalize.
     If we wish to generalize to a larger group of individuals
than those actually studied, there is one very powerful procedure that enables us to do so. This is a procedure for obtaining a representative sample and follows very specific rules.
First, the large group to which we wish to generalize must be
specified in sufficient detail so that every unit is identifiable (in the open classroom example, the unit is each classroom).
Once this is done, each unit (individual or group) is assigned a
number. It makes no difference how the numbers are assigned.
Next, having decided upon the size of sample that we wish, we
enter a table of random numbers (found in many statistics text-
books). We follow a simple procedure for reading off numbers
that identify the particular individuals or groups to be included in our sample. This process is called *random sampling*.
Its essential feature is that all units (individuals or groups)
in the population have an equal chance of being included in the
sample. If this procedure is followed, one is entitled to generalize (within limits) the findings from a particular sample to
the population from which the sample was selected.
     A variation on this process is called cluster random samp-
ling or more commonly, *cluster sampling*. It differs from pure
random sampling only in that groups, rather than individuals are
selected randomly. An example may clarify the distinction.

An investigator wishes to generalize to all third graders in the state of California. If he used pure random procedure, he would identify by name *all* third graders and randomly select individual students. If he used the cluster sample procedure, he would identify all schools having third graders, randomly select *schools*, and include *all* third graders in the selected schools.

As you can see, the cluster sample procedure is much more practical. However, it is not effective unless a sufficiently large number of groups is used. If you were to use as your sample *all* third graders in only two or three randomly selected schools, you can easily see how nonrepresentative your sample would be.

One final variation should be mentioned. It is simply that one can randomly select individuals within the randomly selected groups rather than including everyone. For example, one can select schools at random, classrooms within the schools at random, and students within classrooms at random.

Although inferior to pure random sampling, cluster sampling is very often appropriate in educational research *providing* a sufficiently large number of *groups* is used.

Random sampling is so powerful a technique that anyone designing a study and wishing to generalize his results should try very hard to obtain a random sample. Suppose, however, that this is either impossible or unfeasible due to such factors as time, distance, or money. What then should be done? The researcher should then describe the sample as thoroughly as possible and describe the population to which generalizing seems warranted. In so doing, the researcher, in effect, presents a rationale or argument to support his contention that the sample is representative of the population intended for generalization. This is clearly an inferior procedure, yet it is often the only one possible.

Another approach can be used. Repeat the study using different groups of subjects and in different situations. This is called *replication*. If a study is repeated several times, using different groups of subjects and under different conditions of geography, socioeconomic level, etc., and the results obtained are essentially the same in each case, one can have additional confidence in generalizing the findings. This approach is a valuable one for building a body of knowledge on a particular topic, but is often of little help to an individual investigator.

Returning to the study of the open classroom, let us examine two student descriptions of the sample of classrooms that was used. The first student wrote:

> The sample consisted of classes that were available for observations in schools that would allow us entry. Our sample is approximately twenty-seven elementary classrooms

from five schools, most of which were on an open classroom basis.

The second student wrote:

The sample of twenty-seven classrooms was obtained from five schools in the San Francisco Bay Area that were reputed to have open classrooms. Three of the schools were in urban settings and two were in suburban situations. The schools had at least some classrooms identified by the administration as open. Of the actual classrooms observed, approximately three-fourths were identified as open. Some of the classrooms were multi-age, and others were not. Grades one through six were included with approximately three-fourths of the rooms including grade four and above. The class size ranged from twenty-five to thirty. The schools differed in socioeconomic backgrounds of the students. One school was upper-middle class; two others were generally middle class and the other two contained many students of low to low-middle, socioeconomic classification.

How are these two descriptions different? _____

_____

_____

_____

_____

_____

_____

_____

Describe the population of classrooms that you feel it would be legitimate to generalize to from this sample: _____

_____

_____

_____

_____

_____

_____

_____

_____

_____

    What additional information on the sample would you like to
have? How would you like it described further? _____

_____

_____

_____

_____

_____

_____

_____

    Suppose that the persons conducting this study wished to
generalize to all classrooms in the San Francisco Bay Area. Indicate whether or not you feel this would be justified and state
your reasons:

_____

_____

_____

_____

_____

_____

_____

_____

_____

If you were planning this study and wished to generalize to the population described above (all elementary classrooms in the San Francisco Bay Area), describe in detail how you would go about obtaining your sample:

_____

_____

_____

_____

_____

_____

_____

_____

AUTHOR'S COMMENTS

The second description is much more informative than the first. One cannot generalize with confidence to any population because random sampling was not used. It might be argued that findings could be generalized to elementary schools reputed to be open that are located in heavily populated areas with much variation in socioeconomic level and ethnic background. In so doing one might wish more information on such seemingly important dimensions as teacher age, teacher philosophy, parent attitudes, resources available to the schools, administrator attitudes, and extent of school experience with openness.

It would be extremely questionable to generalize to all elementary classrooms in the San Francisco Bay Area because: (a) only schools reputed to be open were included; and (b) two-thirds of the classrooms were identified as open, a much higher proportion than is true for this population. Thus, we can be fairly certain that these twenty-seven classrooms are not representative of all elementary classrooms in the Bay Area.

There are two ways to select appropriate samples for such a study. The first would be to identify all the classrooms in the defined geographic area within the grade range. They would each be given an identifying number, and the classrooms comprising the sample would be randomly selected by use of a table of random numbers. In this particular study, this procedure would pose a problem if the sample size could not be increased over thirty. One might not get very many classrooms that exhibit a substantial degree of openness because this is a relatively new innovation. If one could use a sample of sixty or seventy classrooms, there would be much less of a problem. In order to relate degree of openness to motivation, it is essential to have classrooms that differ in openness.

The other approach would be to identify not only the classrooms in a particular grade range, but also to indentify them as to degree of openness or perhaps simply as open or traditional. One could then sample randomly within each of these classifications to obtain a sample of say fifteen open and fifteen traditional classrooms and compare these as to degree of student motivation. The difficulties here are that one would need much information at the outset about the degree of openness of any given classroom, and, further, that one must be careful in generalizing not to extrapolate any obtained relationship to include classrooms not falling under one of these two designations. Nevertheless, either of these approaches would be a great improvement upon the sampling procedure that was actually used.

In the vast majority of studies that have been done in education and throughout the behavioral sciences, random samples have not been used. There seem to be two reasons for this. First, there may be insufficient awareness on the part of researchers of the hazards involved in generalizing when one does not have a random sample. The second reason is that of feasibility. In many studies it is simply not feasible for the researcher to invest time, money, or other resources that are necessary to obtain a random sample from a population he wishes to generalize to. Thus, generalizing must depend upon the argument that the sample employed, even though not chosen randomly, is in fact representative of the desired population. Notice that this justification is based upon argumentation rather than on the more powerful technique of random sampling. Whenever making this argument that the sample is representative, it is essential that the sample be described as thoroughly as possible. This distinction between generalizing based on random sampling and on argumentation is crucial.

EXAMPLES OF SAMPLING

In this section, several examples of research in which the author has participated are provided. In none of these instances was random sampling feasible. Following each of the examples, you are asked to evaluate both the adequacy of the description of the samples and the legitimacy of generalizing to the intended population.

Example 1. Example 1 investigated relationships between characteristics of teacher behavior in the classroom, as assessed through rating scales and observation records, and certain personality characteristics of teachers, as assessed through questionnaires and projective tests.

The intended population for the study included all female elementary school teachers (grades K through 6) in the United States. Since the research was viewed as basic research, the intent was to find relationships between teacher personality and classroom behavior that would have wide applicability and would constitute general laws of teacher behavior. It was assumed that relationships between teacher personality and classroom behavior would be essentially the same throughout the elementary grades (an assumption that was later shown to be questionable). It was decided not to include male teachers because the proportion of male teachers at the elementary level was low at the time of the study.

The nature of the study virtually precluded the use of a random sample. Not only was it considered essential to maintain a good deal of personal contact with the teachers, because research of this kind can be threatening, but the classroom observation procedure necessitated that observations be made in each classroom on a number of occasions over a period of time. These considerations, along with the funds and staff time available for the project, precluded use of a sample much larger than 130 teachers and clearly made it impractical to travel throughout the country collecting data on individual teachers in 130 different locations as would have been likely if a random sample had been used. Rather, two separate samples of teachers in two somewhat different settings, although both in the same geographic area, were used. Both samples of teachers were located in the vicinity of Salt Lake City, Utah. Sample one consisted of 83 teachers comprising almost all of the faculties of four elementary schools in Salt Lake City itself. Sample two consisted of 41 teachers all employed in a different school district that included a number of small towns and suburban areas approximately twenty miles from Salt Lake City. This sample included almost the entire faculties of two elementary schools.

The procedure for locating these teachers was the same for both samples. The researcher contacted district officials and after explaining the project and securing cooperation, requested that schools be identified to meet two conditions. The first was that the principal would be supportive of the study and that there were no special problems within the school that would make the collection of data difficult. The second condition was that the schools involved represent the various areas of the community and various backgrounds of the pupils as well as possible. After schools were so identified, meetings were held with each principal; subsequent to his agreement, the researchers met with the entire faculties. The project was described, questions were answered, and the cooperation of the teachers was solicited.

All but four teachers in the city and all but one teacher in the suburban setting cooperated in the research. In both samples virtually the entire range of age and teaching experiences was covered. The city sample comprised four schools representing different neighborhoods and different socioeconomic levels. They also varied from very modern schools with the latest facilities to an old building with much less in the way of facilities. In the second sample, both schools were in a suburban area and served quite similar socioeconomic levels. They can be described as middle-class schools serving residential areas. Most of the parents worked in the nearby city. The two samples of teachers differed in some respects: the relationships among certain of the attributes that we studied were different in the two samples, and the rate of turnover was much higher in the urban setting. On most of the measures obtained, however, the two samples were quite similar.

Evaluate the adequacy of the sample for generalizing to the intended population (page 93):

_____

_____

_____

_____

_____

_____

_____

_____

What additional information would you wish in order to help you judge where the findings of this study might be applicable? Be specific.

_____

_____

_____

_____

_____

_____

_____

_____

_____

AUTHOR'S COMMENTS

Clearly the lack of random sampling makes generalization to the intended population tentative. The information provided on the sample suggests that it may be representative of teachers to be found in many schools throughout this country. Further, some support for generalizing the findings is to be found in the fact that two separate samples that differed in certain respects were used and that the major findings of the research were essentially the same for both samples. (This, of course, could not be known before the study was completed.) A major finding of the study was that the extent to which the teacher exhibited controlling behavior in the classroom was predicted by her score on a questionnaire measure of control need. The fact that a wide variety of age levels, teaching experience, and socioeconomic backgrounds of pupils was included in the samples is a positive feature. On the negative side, it seems likely that the sample used would be different from the total population of elementary teachers in that very few members of ethnic minorities were included in the sample, and no teachers in ghetto areas were included. Finally, it is hazardous to generalize findings to the present from a study that was done, as this one was, ten years ago. This is particularly so with the increased interest in different teaching styles and innovations that is allegedly occurring in the 1970s. One could also argue that teachers in this locale might differ from teachers elsewhere with regard to certain attitudes, expectations, and the like. If this study were to be repeated in a large, metropolitan area containing a large representation of ethnic minorities in a different geographic locale using more recent data and the results were much the same, one would have much more confidence in generalizing the results.

Example 2. In example 2, the sample is described first, after which you will be asked to judge the appropriateness of generalizing to various populations. The purpose of the study was to investigate differences among teachers in their classroom behavior. The same data collection procedures were used in two succeeding years with two samples of teachers, although with some overlap.

Sample one included thirty-three teachers, subdivided into two groups. Group one included eleven first-year teachers, all of whom were graduates of the same training program designed to prepare teachers for inner-city classrooms. The second group consisted of twenty-two experienced teachers in the same schools and grade levels as the first group. Six elementary schools in the San Francisco Bay Area were represented. Four of these were

in urban inner-city schools, and two were in a suburban inte-
grated school district.

Sample two was comprised of fifty-three teachers, all of
whom were teaching in urban, inner-city classrooms. This group
was comprised of fifteen first-year graduates of the training
program, six graduates of the same program in their second year
of full-time teaching, twelve first-year teachers who had gradu-
ated from other programs, twelve experienced teachers in the
same schools as the first-year program teachers, and eight outstanding teachers in the same schools (identified as such by
district personnel). Given this much descriptive information,
indicate the degree of confidence you would have in generalizing
any findings of this study to each of the conceivable populations described below. In each case, state the reasons for your
assessment.

Specified Population	Reason for Judgment

1. All elementary school
    teachers in the United
    States:

    _____   _____

    _____   _____

    _____   _____

    _____   _____

2. All teachers in the San
    Francisco Bay Area:

    _____   _____

    _____   _____

    _____   _____

3. All elementary teachers in
    inner-city schools through-
    out the United States:

    _____   _____

    _____   _____

    _____   _____

Specified Population	Reason for Judgment
4. All elementary teachers in inner-city schools throughout the Bay Area:	_____
	_____
	_____
	_____
5. All elementary teachers in the same schools as those that were involved in the study:	_____
	_____
	_____
	_____
6. All elementary teachers who were graduates of the teacher-training program in question:	_____
	_____
	_____
	_____

What additional information would you need in order to help you decide whether or not the findings could be generalized to any or all the above populations?

_____

_____

_____

AUTHOR'S COMMENTS

The samples are probably not representative of specified populations 1 and 2 with regard to the characteristics of (a) age, (b) teaching experience, (c) educational philosophy, (d) ethnicity, (e) proportion of males, and (f) personality characteristics. Many things affect placement in an inner-city school, including, in many school systems, the routine placing of inexperienced teachers in ghetto schools. Further, the particular geographic location and its likely relationship to (g) attitudes, (h) teaching style, etc., is a further problem in generalizing to population 1. Many of these same limitations apply to population 3, although characteristics (a) to (f) are probably better represented for this population. Although differences in location are undoubtedly of importance, I would be willing to tentatively generalize to population 4 but this is based on personal observations of a variety of schools and hence difficult to defend. Population 5 is probably most legitimate although the sample weighs graduates of a particular program too heavily and is overweighted with new teachers. The particular subgroups of program graduates constitute a fairly good sample for population 6 because they represent a sizeable proportion of employed graduates of the program. Use of other than program graduates would result in very poor representativeness of this population.

Example 3. Example 3 illustrates another common situation with regard to generalizing. The study was not designed to enable generalizing to any explicit population. Rather, it was intended as a program evaluation within a big city school system. Special funds had been provided to a particular school (among others) in the ghetto or target area (in this case meaning a school population predominantly Black with a mixture of low and middle-class socioeconomic groups). Funding of the project itself had come about largely through political efforts on the part of organized parents in the community that was served by the school.

The specific purpose of this study was to assess the outcomes of the special programs instituted in the school after the first year of operation. Although most authorities agree that a one-year period is too short a time in which to attempt a formal evaluation of an educational program, it is clear that this was one of the purposes of the study. A second purpose, however, was to provide a process or formative evaluation, that is, to provide feedback to project participants as to what was happening in the school with the view toward changing those aspects that were less satisfactory. In order to simplify, only part of the total evaluation procedure will be described.

Two different samples were used. The first sample was comprised of students in the school and was used to assess progress in reading, which was one of the primary concerns of the special program. The second sample consisted of the teachers and other adults who worked at the school and was used to assess reactions to many specific aspects of the program. The procedures used in collecting information will be discussed in more detail in chapter four. At this point it is sufficient to indicate that the information from adults was obtained through individual structured interviews and that the information on reading improvement was obtained by using three tests, one of which is pertinent to the present discussion.

The sample of adults was intended to include all adults working in the school. This included: thirty-one teachers; thirty paraprofessionals; fourteen administrative staff including supervising teachers and researchers; and eleven classified staff (custodial, clerical, or cafeteria); a total of eighty-six people. The actual sample included all of these with the exception of one teacher, two paraprofessionals, three administrators, and four cafeteria workers, totalling seventy-six out of the possible eighty-six people. The thirty-one teachers represented a range of age, experience, and educational philosophies. As a group, it was considerably younger, on the average, than might be expected of a typical school. About one-third of the teachers were in their first four years of teaching experience.

Approximately 20 percent of the faculty was Black. The paraprofessional group was approximately 90 percent Black and drawn almost exclusively from the community immediately surrounding and served by the school. Most paraprofessionals were under the age of thirty and represented a wide variety of educational backgrounds. Some were in college and others had considerable difficulty with basic academic skills. With a few exceptions, each paraprofessional was assigned to a particular classroom and in most instances functioned as a second teacher rather than in the more customary role of aide or clerical assistant.

The administrative and professional group, including counselors and administrators, was comprised of individuals of varying backgrounds. Several of the administrators were in their first or second year at the school. Little detailed information was obtained for the classified personnel. They were a somewhat older group for the most part and were approximately 70 percent Black.

The student sample was intended to include all students in grades one through six with kindergarten excluded from the study. There were approximately ninety children at each grade level. In fact, however, the actual sample consisted of 75 to 80 percent of the students at each grade level. The other students were not included, in some cases due to absence and lack of follow-up, but in more instances due to inappropriate testing procedures. Inspection of the test papers of these children suggested that their deletion from the sample, due to inaccurate scores, did not necessarily introduce any systematic distortion. That is, it did not appear that they were either the better or poorer students, or that anything to do with their own performance contributed to the inappropriate procedure that was followed by the tester.

At first glance it might appear that the population for this study was nothing more than the students and adults in the particular school that was studied. However, as is often the case, there were a number of different populations implied in the generalizations that various individuals or groups attempted to make from the study.

Given the above information, evaluate the adequacy of generalizing to the population described in each instance listed below.

1. To all specified inner-city, predominantly Black, and low-income schools in the same city. Although not specifically stated, it was clear from statements made by particular individuals and groups that they intended to generalize findings of the study to this population. For example, it was clear that the school district board of education was interested in the success of this program partly because of the possibility that the same or similar programs might be introduced in other schools of a similar nature.

Your evaluation: _____

_____

_____

_____

_____

2. To all schools of a similar student make-up in selected (or all) large cities throughout the United States. It became evident that generalization to this population was intended by representatives of a private firm that had contracted to provide materials as one aspect of the program.

Your evaluation: _____

_____

_____

_____

3. To Black children in general. It became clear to the
evaluator that certain people hoped that the study would demonstrate that Black children were difficult to teach, and they
hoped to generalize this kind of finding to Black children in
general.

Your evaluation: _____

_____

_____

_____

_____

4. To urban inner-city schools in which the parent community exhibits considerable impact on the school (i.e., community control). It became evident that several groups were hoping
to generalize the results found in this study either to support
or refute the desirability of increased community control over
school affairs.

Your evaluation: _____

_____

_____

_____

_____

What additional information would you wish to have in order
to generalize any findings of this study to any or all of the
above populations?

_____

_____

_____

_____

AUTHOR'S COMMENTS

It is dangerous to generalize findings from this study to any of the populations described above because the unit of sampling here is the school itself and the unit is simply one school. Anyone attempting to generalize from a sample of one is in serious trouble. It is probably impossible to describe all of the characteristics of the school in enough detail so that a reader could decide whether any results could be applied to any other particular school or group of schools. Among other things, one would have to describe something of the history of the school (particularly its recent history), the interpersonal and political interactions within the school, the philosophy and practices of the administration, and the political situation both within the city school system and the community at large. It would also be necessary to have more detailed information on the characteristics of both students and adults in the school. This would include such characteristics as socioeconomic background, which has been shown to be important in relation to the outcomes of academic programs. The findings of this study were of value to the school in question but should not be generalized.

The next assignment is to identify three examples of questionable generalizing from a sample. Take them from your own experience. A good source of examples is the popular media. For example, on a recent late-night television talk-show, a psychiatrist was describing his study of airline hijackers. He described hijackers at some length and pointed out that their outstanding characteristic (which he had discovered by extensive psychiatric interviewing) was a consistent record of failure. His sample consisted of approximately twenty sky-jackers he had interviewed in jail. Although not explicitly stated, it seemed obvious that the population he intended to generalize to was sky-jackers in general. What fallacy do you see in generalizing to this population?

Fallacy: _____

_____

_____

_____

_____

_____

AUTHOR'S COMMENTS

Because there have been many more than twenty sky-jackers (many of them successful), it is clearly unrepresentative to study only those who were caught. Perhaps the outstanding characteristic of successful sky-jackers is their consistent history of success.

As you collect your three examples, keep in mind that what you want are examples of questionable generalizing from one sample of people to a broader population due to lack of representativeness of the sample. A similar process exists when, as we often do, we generalize about an individual based on a small and often unrepresentative sampling of his behavior. Describe your examples of inappropriate generalizing below.

Example 1: Purpose and/or findings of the study: _____

_____

_____

_____

Description of sample: _____

_____

_____

_____

Population (stated or implied) to which a generalization is made: _____

_____

_____

_____

Why is generalizing questionable? _____

_____

_____

_____

Example 2: Purpose and/or findings of the study: _____

_____

_____

_____

Description of sample: _____

_____

_____

_____

Population (stated or implied) to which a generalization is
made: _____

_____

_____

_____

Why is generalizing questionable? _____

_____

_____

_____

Example 3: Purpose and/or findings of the study: _____

_____

_____

_____

Description of sample: _____

_____

_____

_____

Population (stated or implied) to which a generalization is made: _____

_____

_____

_____

Why is generalizing questionable? _____

_____

_____

_____

Next, specify both a population and a procedure for obtaining a sample for the study that you are designing. In defining the population, you must specify the individuals or groups to be included so that you could proceed to identify all such individuals or groups. You should then describe how you would go about selecting a sample for your study, including the size of the sample. It may be that either the nature of your question or practical considerations prevent you from actually carrying through the sampling procedure that you would wish. Nevertheless, for this exercise, design the sampling procedure in the best way you can. If you foresee that this ideal procedure is not feasible, specify how you could in fact obtain a sample in order to collect data for your proposed study. Be specific; you may want to refer back to pages 86, 87, and 93. Following this, state what population you feel you will be entitled to generalize to from your study and why.

Desired population: _____

_____

_____

Ideal sampling procedure (describe in detail): _____

_____

_____

_____

_____

_____

_____

_____

Actual sampling procedure (if same as above, write "same"):

_____

_____

_____

_____

Justifiable population: _____

_____

_____

SUMMARY

In this chapter you have become acquainted with techniques for obtaining a sample that will permit generalizing of
results. You have also seen examples of the cautions necessary
when ideal sampling procedures are not used. This is a good
time to review your total plan, including instrumentation, and
see if the various aspects fit together. Does your instrumentation seem appropriate to the sample you can obtain? Perhaps you
have or will want to revise your hypothesis after thinking
through the problems of instrumentation and sampling. Such revisions are common and are a part of the process of developing
a coherent study.

Our next consideration has to do with arrangements for data collection—the focus of chapter four.

Major concepts considered in this chapter were:

Generalizing results	Random sampling
Population	Cluster sampling
Sample	Replication
Representativeness	

REFERENCES FOR FURTHER READING

Borg, W. G. *Educational Research*. 2d ed. New York, N.Y.: David McKay, 1971. Chap. 8.

Kerlinger, F. N. *Foundations of Behavioral Research*. New York, N.Y.: Holt, Rinehart & Winston, 1964. Chap. 4.

Levine, S. and Elzey, F. F. *A Programmed Introduction to Research*. Belmont, Calif.: Wadsworth, 1968. Chap. 3.

Travers, R. M. W. *An Introduction to Educational Research*. 2d ed. New York, N.Y.: MacMillan, 1964.

Procedures
or "How to Avoid Kidding Yourself"

INTRODUCTION

On completion of this chapter you should be able to recognize and apply basic designs to a research hypothesis. You should be able to examine a study for possible bias and apply procedures for eliminating or reducing such bias. You will have applied both to your own proposed study. You will also have made plans for your pilot study.

The *procedures* in a study consist of the arrangements made for data collection and the design of the study. Arrangements include those required for application of the measuring instrument(s) and any others necessary for data collection. These arrangements may include contacting people, locating the setting for any interviews that are conducted, organizing methods for training observers, etc. It is important in any study that the procedures that are followed in obtaining and treating the data be specified in sufficient detail that another researcher could repeat the study in the same way.

The *design* of a study refers essentially to the way in which a relationship is studied. The two basic forms of design are the single group study, in which a group is described or in which measures of one variable[1] are related to measures on another variable, and the multiple group study, which utilizes two or more groups known to differ on some dimension. These differing groups are then compared on another dimension.

---

[1]The term *variable* is frequently used in research. It is defined as any characteristic that can vary, i.e., take on different degrees of quantity or quality. Classroom openness and arithmetic skill are examples of variables that differ in amount or quantity. Eye color and sex (male-female) are examples of variables differing in quality, not quantity (sex can also be quantitative, or course).

The single group design may be made clearer by reference to
figure 4.1, which pertains to the open classroom study. You
will recall that the two variables studied were the degree of
openness and the degree of student motivation. The relationship

FIGURE 4.1
EXAMPLE OF SINGLE GROUP DESIGN: SCATTERPLOT
USED TO PORTRAY RELATIONSHIP BETWEEN TWO VARIABLES

(Data are only a part of those obtained in the open classroom
study and *do not* represent the actual results.)

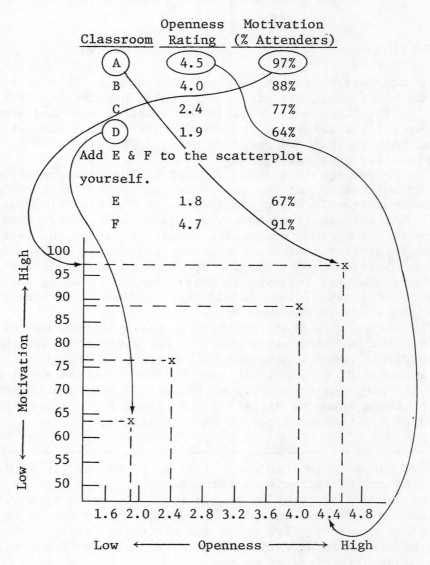

Classroom	Openness Rating	Motivation (% Attenders)
A	4.5	97%
B	4.0	88%
C	2.4	77%
D	1.9	64%

Add E & F to the scatterplot
yourself.

E	1.8	67%
F	4.7	91%

between them may be portrayed graphically. All that is required
is a measurement on each variable for each classroom. Given
these, each classroom may be located on both variables and its
position plotted. The resulting diagram is called a *scatterplot*.
This design is most commonly used when one cannot experimentally
control[2] either variable and where the variables to be studied
lend themselves easily to presentation along a continuum.

Does the scatterplot indicate that a relationship exists?

If so, how would you describe it? _____

_____

_____

Would this relationship support the hypothesis (i.e., the
more open the classroom, the higher the motivation)? Why? Or
why not?

_____

_____

The multiple group design can also be illustrated with the
open classroom study. It would require a group of classrooms
designated as open and a second group designated as less open or
perhaps traditional. Each classroom would be considered the
same as all others in its group for purposes of the study, i.e.,
either open or traditional. Measures of motivation would be obtained, and some basis for comparing the two groups would be
made. A simple means of doing this is to compare the average of
the two groups as illustrated in table 4.1.

Either of these designs (single group or multiple group)
could be used in this study. Notice, however, that the procedure for collecting data would be different for the two designs
(if this is not clear, reread page 92).

---

[2]Discussed in detail later in this chapter.

TABLE 4.1
EXAMPLE OF MULTIPLE GROUP DESIGNS
(Fictitious data.)

	Open Classroom Motivation Score*	Traditional Classroom Motivation Score
	64%	60%
	71%	85%
	57%	79%
	82%	94%
	78%	87%
Sum	352	405
Average	$\frac{352}{5}$ = 70.4%	$\frac{405}{5}$ = 81.0%

*Percentage attenders based on observation record (see page 48).

How much difference is there in the average of the two groups? _____

_____

Would these data support the hypothesis? Why? Or why not?

_____

_____

_____

AUTHOR'S COMMENTS

The scatterplot shows a sizeable relationship between openness and motivation. Classrooms rated high in openness are judged high in motivation. This is what was predicted in the hypothesis and hence provides support for it.

The comparison of averages shows a difference of 10.6 points. These data would not *support the hypothesis because the hypothesis predicted high motivation in the open classrooms whereas these (fictitious) data show higher motivation in the traditional classrooms.*

The procedures actually followed in the open classroom study were as follows: the sample of twenty-six classrooms was contained in five schools. Eighteen observers were divided into nine teams of two observers each. The number of teams visiting each school was determined primarily by school size and varied from one to six. Each team except one (see page 85) observed three classrooms selected to include at least one classroom identified as traditional (if there was one in the school). All observations were done during the same week and most were done on the same midweek day. Prior to arriving, each school was called by one of the observers, and the time of the visit was arranged.

Each classroom was visited once for a period of thirty to forty minutes. During this time the two observers completed both the rating scale for openness and the observation record of motivation (attention).[3]

After completing the observation, each observer averaged his ratings to obtain a score on openness for the *classroom* and averaged the number of attenders across the six five-minute intervals to obtain the measure of motivation. Comparison of the values obtained by the two observers in each classroom provided an index of observer agreement. The measures were averaged for the two observers to obtain the final measure of openness and motivation for each classroom. These measures were portrayed in a scatterplot in order to test the hypothesis.[4] This is to say, the single group (of classrooms) design was used.

---

[3] This is an extremely weak part of the procedure because it is unlikely that reliable measurements can be obtained from only one observation period (see page 46).

[4] Additional details on instrument development and obtaining the sample are not included here since they were presented in chapters two and three.

CONTAMINATION

Sometimes a study is designed and carried out in such a way
that, while the researcher feels that his data support or refute
his hypothesis, the data may not have provided an adequate test
of the hypothesis at all. There are several ways in which this
can happen. Two of them have already been considered: the use
of unreliable or invalid measuring devices and use of an unrepresentative sample. In addition a study may be rendered inade-
quate because of contamination due to: the effects of extraneous
variables; and procedural bias. Following is a discussion of
each.

Extraneous Variables. The problem of extraneous variables
can be illustrated by the old story of "The Dog Who Barked the
Sun Up!" A dog made some interesting observations relating his
barking and the appearance of the sun. Each morning after wak-
ing, his barking was followed shortly by the appearance of the
sun. "Obviously," there was a relationship between his barking
and the appearance of the sun; how marvelous to be responsible
for its appearance. Clearly, the dog was mistaken—due to ig-
norance of the operation of other variables. This problem is
particularly acute when, as in this example, one attempts to
establish that one series of events *causes* a second series of
events. But the problem is present in any study.
Consider, for example, our ubiquitous open classroom study.
What we intended to study was the relationship between the degree of openness in a classroom and the level of student motivation. Our procedure was to visit a number of classrooms and
obtain measurements intended to reflect these two variables.
Subsequently we wished to determine whether a high degree of
classroom openness tended to go with a high degree of student
motivation. Let us assume that such a relationship was found,
thereby supporting the hypothesis. The question still remains:
"Were other factors involved that affected this relationship?"
Suppose that the more open classrooms were all found in affluent
schools where more materials and activities for students were
provided. If this were the case, the higher motivation in these
classrooms might be attributable to the supply of materials and
not to the openness of teaching style. In such a situation the
supply of materials would be considered an extraneous variable.
It was able to influence the outcome of the study and mislead
the researcher as to the nature of the relationship between
openness and motivation.
An *extraneous variable*, then, is a variable that affects a
study but is unintended and only serves to distort the findings
and mislead the investigator. Reread the description of the

procedures for the open classroom study and list below other
variables that could conceivably have been operating as extraneous variables in that study.

Extraneous variables: _____

_____

_____

_____

_____

_____

_____

AUTHOR'S COMMENTS

Many factors could be listed here. One is the possibility that teachers in the more open classrooms were more skillful teachers, independent of the style of teaching, and consequently had more highly motivated students. Another extraneous variable might be the socioeconomic level of the student. If socioeconomic level is related to student motivation and if the more open classrooms were in the more favored socioeconomic brackets, then this would function as an extraneous variable.

Techniques for getting rid of (controlling) the effects of extraneous variables are needed. The most powerful technique that has been devised is *experimentation*. In experimentation the investigator manipulates one (or more) of the variables or dimensions that he is studying. Rather than *finding* differing degrees of a particular variable, the experimenter *creates* them. In the open classroom example, this would mean manipulating classrooms to create differing degrees of openness. In its simplest form, this would require creating two groups of classrooms that differ in their degree of openness. This could, of course, be extended to creating three, four, or more groups differing along a continuum of openness. The fact that the experimenter has deliberately created these conditions enables him to have additional confidence that the classrooms are truly different with regard to the variable that is being studied. If, in addition to manipulating the variable, the experimenter can also assign individuals randomly to his two or more conditions or treatments, a very favorable research position has been created—a true experiment.

Suppose that a researcher defined three degrees of openness in the classroom and created several classrooms of each degree. This might require systematically arranging furniture, providing for various activities, and training teachers (randomly assigned) in the teaching style appropriate to each degree of openness. Then suppose that students were assigned on a purely random basis to the three treatments. If the groups are large enough, the researcher can be fairly confident that systematic differences in the degree of openness have been created and that no other variables are able to contaminate the experiment. Any other variable that is related to student motivation should be balanced out in the three treatment groups. Thus such variables as socioeconomic level of students, ability of the students, competence of the teacher, or resources provided should not differ systematically from one group to another. If it is found that the three treatment groups differ with regard to the degree of student motivation, one can be relatively confident in

attributing these differences to different degrees of openness
in the classroom.

Although this method is by far the most effective in rul-
ing out possible contamination in a study, its major limitation
is the difficulty of putting it into practice. For most research in education, it is difficult to arrange for systematic
manipulation of a particular variable. It is, perhaps, even
more difficult to arrange for students, teachers, or other individuals to be assigned randomly to differing conditions.
There are many reasons for this difficulty. The fact is that
our educational institutions are not set up for research purposes even though they may protest otherwise. Consider the
problem facing a principal who wishes to assign his ninety
third-graders on a random basis to three different classrooms.
He will immediately be subjected to pressure from students,
teachers, and parents, all wanting certain placements for particular reasons.

Another reason experimentation of this form is rarely used
is the difficulty in specifying the precise conditions one
wishes to create. Recall the difficulty in defining the characteristics of the open classroom, and you will appreciate how
difficult it would be to specify precisely how the most open
classroom should be arranged both in terms of physical apparatus
and style of teaching. Finally, it may be questioned whether
certain conditions *can* be created. For example, could teachers
be trained to carry out the specifications of an open classroom
if they were randomly assigned to do so?

As a result of all these difficulties, experimenters often
conduct laboratory studies in which they can more precisely control the conditions. An example is the study of rote memory
under highly controlled conditions such as sound controlled
rooms and one-to-one instruction. The main criticism of such
studies is the difficulty of generalizing from the laboratory to
the school. Consequently, much experimental research in psychology and education is criticized as being artificial.

A variation of experimentation consists of systematically
manipulating one variable but without random assignment of individuals to the varying conditions. This quasi-experimental
procedure is clearly inferior to the experimental procedure described previously, but it does give the researcher some additional control over extraneous variables.

If the researcher is not in a position to manipulate or
create differing conditions, he has several options. First, he
may control certain variables that are known (or thought) to influence what he is studying by holding them *constant*. For example, if in the open classroom study we were concerned with the
possible contaminating effect of differing grade levels, one approach would be to conduct the study entirely at a particular

grade level. Thus, if second-graders are more highly motivated
than fifth-graders, one can remove this particular influence by
studying only fifth-graders. Although this technique is quite
effective for controlling particular variables, it is limited.
The researcher can never be sure that he has controlled all pertinent variables through this technique. Furthermore, if one
attempts to control more than a few variables in this way, one
rapidly cuts down on the size of the sample.

A second technique is to collect measurements on extraneous
variables that are known (or thought) to influence the variables
being studied. Thus, if it is not feasible to control these
variables by holding them constant, one can often measure them
and investigate the degree to which they are influencing a particular study. For example, in the open classroom study, if one
needed to study classrooms across different grades, one could
find out whether or not grade level is related to motivation by
seeing if the average motivation score was different for different grades. If little or no relationship is found, this variable is probably of little consequence. We need not be worried
about nor control variables that are unrelated to what we are
studying. For example, we would not bother to determine differing heights of the teachers in our various classrooms, because
we would assume that height of the teacher is unrelated to the
degree of motivation of the student.

Another technique that is employed to control extraneous
variables is that of *matching*. Information on certain variables
that the investigator wishes to control is obtained and used to
match individuals in the differing groups so that the groups are
equated. This technique can only be used if one is using a
multiple group design. Although this technique is useful in
many instances, it too suffers from limitations. First, as with
the technique of holding the variable constant, one soon finds
it difficult in practice to match even two groups on more than a
few variables. Second, in order to effect good matching, it is
sometimes necessary to exclude individuals at the extremes of
one of the extraneous variables. If one wished to compare a
group of Cerebral Palsy children with normal groups of children
regarding certain personality characteristics, one might wish
to control for tested academic ability. In so doing, one could
match individuals in the two groups but would certainly end up
with samples that would not be typical of one or the other group
of children since it is known that the average of tested academic ability for Cerebral Palsy children is considerably lower
than for normal children. Thus one would have to limit conclusions to the range of scores used in matching.

It should be mentioned at this point that there are statistical procedures that can sometimes be used to achieve many of
the controls previously discussed. The principle techniques

here are called analysis of variance and analysis of covariance.
For present purposes, it is sufficient that you be aware that it
is possible to design a study in such a way that extraneous variables can be controlled (their influence be eliminated) through
combinations of matching and statistical analysis.

It is essential in conducting any study that the investigator give attention to the possible contaminating effects of uncontrolled, extraneous variables. An attempt should be made to
identify all such possible variables and either control them or
investigate their effects within the study. Of course, one cannot possibly do this for every conceivable variable. Consequently, it must be acknowledged that any individual study (other
than a classic experimental study using a large sample) may be
subject to the criticism that some uncontrolled variables may be
contaminating the findings. The best solution to this problem
is repetition of the study in other settings and preferably by
other investigators.

Procedural Bias. Another problem plaguing the researcher
is the possibility that a bias or distortion is introduced into
his study, not through the operation of some outside variable
that has not been controlled, but rather through some distortion
that is built into his procedures. An example as applied to the
open classroom study is the possibility that the presence of observers in the classroom introduces some sort of systematic distortion. It is conceivable that in the less open classroom, the
presence of an observer is more noticeable and hence more dis-
tracting. In such a case, if lower motivation were observed in
the less open classroom, it might be due to this distraction
rather than the degree of openness of the classroom. The possibilities for introducing this kind of bias are endless. A few
of the more common types are as follows:

• Characteristics of the interviewer in studies that rely
upon the interview for collecting data can affect responses.
Since the main feature of the interview method is person to person contact, it is evident that the interaction between the interviewer and the respondent may affect the answers that are obtained. This is particularly likely if the interviewer differs
from the interviewee in significant ways related to the topic of
the interview. For example, it is probable that men and women
interviewers would get different responses when interviewing in
relation to the Women's Liberation Movement.

• The setting in which interviewing is done may have some
bearing on the answers. One of the limitations of the interviews that were done assessing children's opinions of their
classrooms (page 53) was that the interviews were conducted in
class and frequently other children were nearby and sometimes

intruded into the interview. This may have affected how particular children answered.

    ● Whenever instruments are not administered as intended, an
important source of procedural bias is introduced. This, of
course, serves to lessen the validity of the measurements. In
addition to decreasing validity, however, this factor may introduce a systematic bias into a study. An example is teachers in
a special program allowing their students extra time on a test.

    ● Attitudes of the data collector can be another source of
procedural bias. If, for example, teachers or test administrators in low economic or ethnic minority schools communicate to
students that they expect them to do poorly on a test, this may
produce anxiety or anger in some children and result in their
performing more poorly than they would otherwise. If these
schools are compared to others in which the tester attitude is
different, this systematic bias will distort the findings.

    Can you list other types of procedural bias that can occur?

_____

_____

_____

_____

_____

    Techniques for dealing with procedural bias fall into the
following general categories:

    a) Standardize procedures (e.g., do interviewing in the
same setting; write out test directions).

    b) Select and/or train investigators.

    c) Allow for an adjustment period before collecting data
(e.g., establish rapport with the interviewee, visit classrooms
once or twice before making records).

    d) Plan for ignorance. Since knowledge about subjects,
instruments, procedures, or hypotheses may cause bias, it is
often desirable to keep data gatherers in the dark on such mat-
ters. Thus, the researcher may even take steps to prevent himself from knowing which classroom is experimental or which pa-
tient received the sugar pill instead of the drug.

    e) Collect information on potential sources of bias (e.g.,
tape interview to see if interviewers behave differently).

    Your next assignment is to specify the procedures that you
would follow in conducting your study. Try to design the best
procedure you can. At the same time, keep it within the realm
of feasibility. A good frame of reference may be to think of

having a small grant that would provide assistance and a time period of about one year. Describe *in detail* the procedures that you would follow within each of the following headings:

Your hypothesis: _____

_____

_____

Selecting subjects (how will you identify your sample?):

_____

_____

_____

_____

_____

Soliciting cooperation of persons involved: _____

_____

_____

_____

_____

_____

Situational manipulations introduced, if any (what special conditions must be set up?): _____

_____

_____

_____

_____

_____

Collecting data (who will collect it and how?): _____

_____

_____

_____

_____

Design (how will you study your hypothesized relationship?;

see page 111): _____

_____

_____

_____

_____

_____

SOURCES OF BIAS

Although there are many specific sources of bias that may affect a particular study, it is helpful to categorize them under certain broad headings. One such listing is adapted from Campbell and Stanley[5] (numbers 1 through 5 are extraneous variables; numbers 6 through 9 are procedural variables). Later, we will apply these categories to specific examples.

1. *Subject Selection*. The selection of people for a study may result in the individuals or groups differing from one another in unintended ways that are related to the variables to be studied. Example: The classrooms selected as differing in openness might also differ systematically in ability level of the students, which might well affect their level of motivation.

---

[5]Campbell, D. T., and Stanley, J. C., "Experimental and Quasi-Experimental Designs for Research on Teaching," in N. L. Gage, ed., *Handbook of Research on Teaching* (Chicago: Rand McNally, 1963). Originally copyrighted by American Educational Research Association, Washington, D.C.

2.   *Loss of Subjects*.   If during the course of a study, individuals or groups of subjects are lost to the researcher, this
may introduce a systematic bias.   This is particularly a problem
in questionnaire studies where it is customary for 10 to 20 percent or more of the subjects not to return their questionnaires.
Because it is probable that this failure to respond is related
to the questions asked, this loss of subjects is likely to introduce bias.   Example: In the open classroom study, if the researcher were denied access to certain classrooms, a systematic
bias would probably be introduced.

3.   *Location Selection*.   The particular setting in which
data is collected may affect results in unintended ways.   Example: The classrooms selected as more open might have more resources (supplies, parent support, etc.) available to them.
This variable might have an influence on student motivation.

4.   *Extraneous Events*.   Unanticipated events may take place
during the course of data collection that affect the results.
Example: In the open classroom study, an announcement might be
made that prizes will be offered to the hardest working classrooms.   Such an announcement made only in certain open classrooms could affect the level of student motivation.   This problem is of greater magnitude when the study is carried out over
a longer period of time, as when one introduces some form of
long-term treatment that is then evaluated.

5.   *Maturation*. Maturation refers to differences in individuals or groups that occur due to natural or expected growth
over the passage of time.   Example: In the open classroom study,
maturation would cause bias if the open classrooms tended to
have either older or younger children in them (due to the time
of year when they were observed) and if the degree of aging was
related to motivation.   Again, this problem is greatest in studies carried out over a long period of time.

6.   *Attitude of Subjects*.   The way in which subjects view
the study and their participation in it can be a source of bias.
The attitude of subjects is likely to be influenced by the way
in which they are solicited for participation, the instructions
or directions that they are given, the rationale or explanation
used to justify their participation, the setting in which the
research is conducted, and the general demeanor of the members
of the data collection team.   These factors, can, of course, operate to reduce the validity of whatever measures are obtained.
They may also introduce a systematic bias.   Example: In the open
classroom study, if certain observers were viewed as offensive
by the teachers or students, this could introduce a bias if those

individuals tended to visit predominantly open or traditional classrooms. This is of more concern when subjects are asked to participate directly in a particular procedure than when they are observed.

A special case of this problem, which is of considerable importance, is the so-called Hawthorne Effect. This term refers to a phenomenon first observed in the Hawthorne plant of Western Electric. The workers improved in their output whenever they were given a special treatment regardless of the nature of that treatment. Thus, it may be expected that whenever a group of people is singled out for a special curriculum or other form of treatment, there will be a tendency for them to perform in ways judged as better by the researcher as a result of this special consideration and not necessarily due to the treatment itself.

7. *Objectivity of Data Collection*. Objectivity refers to the possibility (mentioned in chapter one) that the investigator may unconsciously distort his data gathering procedures in such a way as to support his hypothesis. Example: In the open classroom study, the fact that the same observers were assessing the openness of the classroom and the degree of student motivation could lead to bias since their ratings of openness might affect their perception of motivation level. There are many ways of dealing with this problem. All of them essentially serve to prevent the investigator from having this kind of control of the data. In our example, one technique would be to train one group of observers to judge the openness of the classrooms and a second group to judge the degree of motivation, with neither group acquainted with the hypothesis to be tested. The basic rules to be followed are: (a) the data gathering procedure for differing measures should be kept independent; and (b) the individual collecting the data should either not be aware of the hypothesis being tested or should be unable to identify the particular subjects or groups on whom data is obtained with regard to other than the particular variable being assessed.

8. *Effects of Sequential Measurement*. Any study in which measurements are taken over a period of time must be concerned about the effects of the measuring process on the people or situations being measured. Presumably this is a minor problem in studies using direct observation, but more of a problem whenever subjects are asked to participate through taking tests, answering questions, etc. The very experience of participating in these ways may affect subsequent measurements. Example: Asking children to respond to questions about their classrooms may have an effect upon their responses to similar questions if repeated at a future date. Once again, this is primarily a problem with a study that uses an assessment of this kind on a before and after basis.

9. *Instrument Decay*. It is possible for the instrumentation process to deteriorate during a study. Tests may become marked up, interviewers may become fatigued, and observers may become bored.

IDENTIFICATION OF BIAS

In this section you will find descriptions of two research projects in which the author participated. In each example, the basic procedure that was followed in the study is described. Your task is to identify possible sources of bias. The categories presented above can serve as a useful checklist. You are asked to examine these studies in the light of each of these categories in turn and identify any possible sources of bias.

Example 1. An elementary school program (this study is the one mentioned in the material on sampling on page 100) was studied to evaluate the effectiveness of a new program in an inner-city elementary school. There were two samples involved. The first sample consisted of all the children in the school except kindergartners. The second consisted of all the adults employed in the school. This discussion is confined to the assessment of reading improvement by means of tests for the children and the assessment of attitudes toward the program on the part of the adults through individual interviews.

Early in the school year school district personnel contacted the evaluator and arrangements were made for the evaluation. The evaluator met with the faculty of the school at a faculty meeting, and the general purpose and procedure of the evaluation were presented. Time was given for questions and discussion. Since an evaluation committee already existed at the school—comprised of teachers, administrators, paraprofessionals, and parents—the evaluator attended regular meetings with this committee at two-week intervals throughout the school year. The evaluation procedures used stemmed from these deliberations.

Reading comprehension was assessed by means of two tests. The first was the Stanford Achievement Test, a well-known and widely used test containing two sections. The first is word meaning in which the student picks the appropriate word to complete a sentence. The second section is paragraph meaning in which the student makes appropriate choices of words to fit into a paragraph. Although this test has a good deal to commend it, especially from the technical standpoint, its format and content have been frequently criticized as not being appropriate for inner-city, minority children.

The second test (labeled Reading Test 2) requires the student to read a passage and then answer a multiple choice question about it. This test was designed specifically to overcome objections to currently used standardized tests. It is a power test; that is, it begins with very short simple sentences and increases in length and complexity of the passages. It consists of ten pages with no more than four passages per page. The pages are not assembled into a booklet. It is administered by the teacher to whatever size groups seem appropriate. Each child receives one page at a time. The teacher begins with pages that the child can read easily (with the exception of some first-graders) and continues until the child answers two questions incorrectly on one page, at which point the testing is terminated. The first (easiest) pages are printed in primary type. The teacher does not present the material as a test, but rather as a sequence of work sheets. In taking the test the child reads each passage, then reads the question and circles the word that answers it correctly.

This test was designed to provide a situation within which the child can best demonstrate his proficiency in reading comprehension with an absence of excessive competition or anxiety. This objective seems to have been achieved, since many teachers and children reported a positive reaction to this test. This advantage was balanced, however, by the fact that it became evident from examining answer sheets and from observation that many teachers were not giving the test according to the directions. Some teachers were not starting the child at an appropriate place or they were not continuing the test long enough or they were providing direct help to the children. Detailed instructions had been provided to each teacher along with a demonstration of the procedure for test administration. However, it became apparent that insufficient attention was given to the preparation of the teachers.

Reading Test 2 was given on a prepost (before and after) basis. It was administered first in early November and again during the last three weeks in May. The results for approximately 20 percent of the pupils at each grade level were unuseable largely due to inappropriate test administration and, for a much smaller number, absence from school. The Stanford Achievement Test was administered early in May to virtually all students.

The interviewing of adults was conducted during a two-week period in the middle of April. The questions to be asked were formulated by the evaluation committee. An introductory statement was prepared that explained the purpose of the interview as being the assessment of the opinions of the adults in the school in relation to the program as it had functioned during the year. The structured interview probed many topics. In the first part, the respondent was asked his judgment about particular aspects of the program such as the use of paraprofessionals. The respondent was asked to first state what he viewed as the positive features of each topic and second to state the negative features. Finally he was asked to rate each topic in one of four categories: excellent, good, fair, or poor. A total of sixteen topics were queried in this fashion. Next the respondent was asked to respond in any way he wished regarding the eight ancillary services provided to the school. This was followed by specific questions such as: "How have you supplemented or deviated from the materials that were provided?" The last section asked the respondent to rate several characteristics of the pupils as excellent, good, fair, or poor and also to compare them with previous years. An example of a pupil characteristic was "attitude toward learning." The interview took approximately one hour per respondent. Each of the adults in the school was scheduled for a specific appointment and during that time was relieved of other responsibilities. Interviews were obtained for seventy-seven of the eighty-six adults in the school.

In the space provided below list all of the potential sources of bias that you can locate. Examine the study from the standpoint of each category. You may conclude that some categories do not constitute a problem. In some cases, you would need more information to judge whether a problem existed.[6] The purpose here is to list as many *possible* sources of bias as you can.

1. Subject selection: Children: _____

_____

_____

Adults: _____

_____

_____

2. Loss of subjects: Children: _____

_____

_____

_____

[6]In some cases you have not been given all the information in order to make this learning experience more valuable.

Adults: _____

_____

_____

3. Location selection: Children: _____

_____

_____

Adults: _____

_____

_____

4. Extraneous Events: Children: _____

_____

_____

Adults: _____

_____

_____

5. Maturation: Children: _____

_____

_____

Adults: _____

_____

_____

6. Attitude of subjects: Children: _____

_____

_____

Adults: _____

_____

_____

7.   Objectivity of data collection: Children: _____

_____

_____

Adults: _____

_____

_____

8.   Effects of sequential measurement (on subjects):
Children: _____

_____

_____

Adults: _____

_____

_____

9.   Instrument decay: Children: _____

_____

_____

Adults: _____

_____

_____

10. Other: Children: _____

_____

_____

Adults: _____

_____

_____

AUTHOR'S COMMENTS

1.   **Subject selection:** *Because the study is viewed strictly as an evaluation of this school, there seems to be no bias introduced by the procedure since all of the people in the school were planned to be included (except kindergarten).   Generalizing beyond this school would be very questionable due to the many difficulties discussed in chapter three.*

2.   **Loss of subjects:** *This was a problem because about 20 percent of the students were lost on the experimental reading test, and approximately 10 percent of the adult interviews were lost to the study.   If those lost were different from the remainder, a bias is introduced.*

3.   **Location selection:** *Same as 1.   All classrooms were included except kindergarten.*

4.   **Extraneous events:** *It is conceivable that external events may have influenced both the amount of gain in pupil reading and the opinions stated by the adults.   For example, improvement in reading could be caused by such factors as Sesame Street viewing.   There could be external conditions, such as the current political situation in a ghetto area, that might de-crease student learning.*

With regard to adults, one can speculate that a variety of external conditions may have contributed to people portraying the program in a favorable or unfavorable light (e.g., employ-ment possibilities at the time or personal interactions in the community).   This is a problem only if one is using the respond-ents' opinions as a valid index of actual program functioning. If, instead, their responses are viewed strictly as reflecting their opinions, regardless of the reasons, then this is much less a problem to the investigator.

5.   **Maturation:** *It is, of course, to be expected that pu-pils will show improvement in reading over a six-month period simply due to maturation.   Thus, what appear to be gains due to the program may be attributable strictly to maturation.   This is unlikely to be a factor in the adult interviews.*

6.   **Attitude of subjects:** *A question can be raised with respect to the attitude of the children toward the tests that they were given.   If the testing was viewed negatively, it might well result in the test not being taken properly.   If, on the other hand, students wished to have their school appear in a very favorable light, this might lead to a propensity for cheat-ing.*

The attitude of the adults interviewed would certainly be expected to affect the forthrightness of their responses.   In any program that has been identified as special and particularly one that has received special funding, one must be concerned about the tendency of persons participating in the program to consciously or unconsciously report it in a favorable light. There is also the possibility of the Hawthorne Effect operating in that any improvements may be attributable only to the special nature of the project, and not to the specifics of the program. An additional issue in this study is raised with respect to the willingness of the Black adults in the school, particularly the paraprofessionals, to be open and frank with the investigator, a Caucasian from a nearby university. Further, one might expect a reluctance on the part of professional personnel to make disparaging remarks that conceivably could find their way into a personnel file. Finally, the attitude of the adults in the school is of great importance since the teachers and paraprofessionals administered the reading tests. Their attitude toward being evaluated and toward the testing procedures is a possible source of bias.

    7.   Objectivity of data collection: A possible bias is introduced by the fact that on the reading test the teachers administered both tests. The teachers had a vested interest in making the test gain look good and this conceivably could have led to their administering the tests in a nonobjective way (e.g., helping students). Another potential problem is in the behavior of the interviewer. It has been demonstrated that interviewers can influence responses by their demeanor and by the way in which questions are asked.

    8.   Effects of sequential measurement: As the same form of Reading Test 2 was administered twice (November and May), it is conceivable that specific carry-over from the first testing could be responsible for some amount of gain in scores.

    9.   Instrument decay: This is not a problem with regard to testing since test materials were used only one time, but could be a problem with regard to the interviewer. An interviewer at the end of eight hours of interviewing may function differently than he did first thing in the morning.

    10.   Other: A variable that does not fit neatly into the above categories is the time of day in which assessment is made. Many teachers are of the opinion that student test performance is affected by the time of day they are tested. It is further possible that a respondent's answers to the interview situation would differ depending on whether they were interviewed first thing in the morning or at the end of a tiring day. Either of these could introduce a bias.

What ways can you think of to eliminate, minimize, or at least clarify the extent of the possible bias in each category that has been identified by you and the author?

1. Subject selection: _____

_____

_____

_____

_____

2. Loss of subjects: _____

_____

_____

_____

3. Location selection: _____

_____

_____

_____

_____

4. Extraneous events: _____

_____

_____

_____

_____

5. Maturation: _____

_____

_____

_____

_____

6. Attitude of subjects: _____

_____

_____

_____

_____

7. Objectivity of data collection: _____

_____

_____

_____

_____

8. Effects of sequential measurement (on subjects): _____

_____

_____

_____

_____

9. Instrument decay: _____

_____

_____

_____

_____

10. Other: _____

_____

_____

_____

_____

AUTHOR'S COMMENTS

Compare your solutions to those actually used.
    *1.   Subject selection: There is no way to deal with the
problems raised by generalizing beyond this school without having additional samples of similar schools.*
    *2.   Loss of subjects: Loss of students due to absence could
introduce a bias if they were students who had achieved either
more or less gain than the students who remained. A check was
not made—although it would have been possible—to obtain some
data on the proficiency of those students. A better procedure
would have been to conduct a follow-up testing program to insure
that all students were included. The main body of students who
were lost, however, were lost due to inappropriate test administration and hence a partial record of their performance was
available. A study of these records supported the view that
neither the best nor the poorest students had been mistested, so
it seemed likely that this loss of students had not resulted in
a bias.*
    *Of the nine adult interviews that were lost, four were due
to technical malfunctioning of equipment that should not result
in a bias. Of the remaining five, one was an administrator who
was unable to schedule an appropriate time; and four were food
service, clerical, and custodial staff who stated that they had
few opinions about the program since it was unrelated to their
duties. It would appear that little bias was introduced due to
loss of these additional five interviews.*
    3.   Location selection: Same as 1.
    *4.   Extraneous events: There was no attempt made in this
study to control the possibility of external events affecting
the child's growth in reading. With regard to adult interviews,
one cannot rule out the possibility of bias. Factors external
to the program itself may have affected the respondents' assessment of it.*
    *5.   Maturation: This problem was handled in two ways. The
first was by comparing scores on Reading Test 2 to data from
other school settings that provided a basis for assessing the
magnitude of gain to be expected, assuming that the different
schools were comparable. The second method was to compare
scores on the standardized test to results from previous years
at the same school. This assumes that the pupils in the school
the year of the study were, at the beginning of the year, no
different from those in previous years. If these assumptions
hold, these techniques give fairly effective control of maturation because the proficiency or gain to be expected can be compared with that achieved.*
    *6.   Attitude of subjects: This problem was dealt with pri-
marily through the evaluation committee in the school. It*

contained representatives from all segments of the school staff and in fact made the decisions as to what and how evaluation would be done. It also served as a means of facilitating communication with the rest of the staff. This appeared to contribute to a generally positive reaction to the evaluation activities on the part of the staff that was presumably passed on to the pupils.

There were no signs of outward antagonism toward the evaluation procedures by either teachers or pupils. Nevertheless, one would have to expect that at least some pupils reacted negatively to the standardized reading test because that was the customary reaction. The reaction to the experimental reading test appeared to be much more positive. It must also be said, however, that some of the errors in test administration may have been due to negative attitudes on the part of teachers or paraprofessionals. The design of this study did not rule out the possibility of a Hawthorne Effect operating. However, the general lack of dramatic success of special programs in schools suggests that the Hawthorne Effect may not operate in that setting.

With regard to adult interviews, the committee tried to arrange interview conditions so that respondents would answer truthfully. Accordingly, each respondent was given assurances that all comments would be kept confidential and that the transcribed responses would be seen only by the evaluator. In addition, it was decided to have Black interviewers interview paraprofessionals, while the evaluator and another Caucasian interviewed the teachers. Both groups interviewed administrators and staff. Each interviewer made comments on the apparent attitude of the interviewee and, with a few exceptions, reported that the respondent, at least to all appearances, was responding without defensiveness or deviousness. One indication that the responses were forthright is the finding that some aspects of the program were viewed almost unanimously as very positive, whereas others were viewed as extremely negative.

7. **Objectivity of data collection:** The study attempted to insure objectivity of testing by training the teachers and paraprofessionals in test administration. However, the data suggest that at least in some cases this condition was not met. However, the failure to adhere to testing instructions appeared to penalize as many children as it helped so that a bias does not seem likely.

The problem of interviewer objectivity was handled by having a completely structured interview with each question spelled out in detail and the interviewer directed not to add to these questions. The fact that interviews were taped made it possible to check on this procedure. It was found that the interviewers followed the directions very carefully. This check, however, *does not eliminate the possibility of bias due to nonverbal cues of some sort.*

8. **Effects of sequential measurement:** *This factor could not be completely ruled out since test data were not available for other students who had been tested at precisely the same dates as in this study. However, by extrapolating from other data that were available, some adjustment for possible effects of test taking was possible; that is, the amount of gain in score to be expected over a six-month interval was calculated for each grade level. It was not possible to separate this factor from the maturation factor; both were handled in the same way.*

9. **Instrument decay:** *The comments made previously with regard to the tapes of the interviewers suggest that this problem was not an important one in this study.*

10. **Other:** *The possible effect of time of day was controlled with regard to the children by instructing teachers to test early in the morning. Regarding the time of interviewing, the interviewer was instructed at the outset of the interview to ask whether this had been an unusual day, and if the respondent indicated that it had been a particularly trying day, the interview was rescheduled. This offered a partial control of the problem.*

Example 2. The purpose of this study was to assess the effects of an innovative curriculum in social studies at the elementary school level. The basic design was the comparison of ten sixth-grade classrooms using the curriculum with ten other sixth-grade classrooms not using the curriculum (an example of the multiple group design). Since the curriculum requires a style of teaching that is somewhat unique, it was necessary that the teachers in the curriculum classrooms have special training. Eight of the curriculum teachers were located in the San Francisco Bay Area; the remaining two were located in a residential suburb of Portland, Oregon. A wide range of pupil characteristics and school environments were represented. One classroom contained predominantly Black children in an inner-city school; a second contained a sizeable proportion of Mexican-American children and was predominantly of lower economic status. At the other economic extreme were several classrooms in affluent, exclusively white, residential settings. Nine different schools were represented. The comparison group of classrooms was selected entirely from one suburban school district with seven elementary schools represented.

Instrumentation consisted of a series of tests given early in the school year and again near the end of the school year. Several of these tests were designed specifically to assess

objectives of the curriculum. An example of these tests was
presented in chapter two (Application of Generalization Test).
In addition, a widely used standardized test was administered
(The STEP Social Studies Test). For each of the tests the hypothesis was that the curriculum classrooms would show greater
gain.

Using the above description, write in the space provided
all the possible sources of bias that you can detect within each
of the categories listed.

1. Subject selection: _____

_____

_____

_____

_____

2. Loss of subjects: _____

_____

_____

_____

_____

3. Location selection: _____

_____

_____

_____

_____

4. Extraneous events: _____

_____

_____

_____

_____

5. Maturation: _____

_____

_____

_____

_____

6. Attitude of subjects: _____

_____

_____

_____

_____

7. Objectivity of data collection: _____

_____

_____

_____

_____

8. Effects of sequential measurement (on subjects): _____

_____

_____

_____

9. Instrument decay: _____

_____

_____

_____

_____

   10. Other: _____

_____

_____

_____

_____

AUTHOR'S COMMENTS

Compare your points to those of the author.

1. Subject selection: Although the principle subjects, the students, were not selected at random, there does appear to be a wide cross section of student characteristics that should entitle some confidence in generalizing to the general population of students. If should be kept in mind, however, that the sample is somewhat weighted toward suburbia and the more affluent strata of our society.

With regard to the comparison of curriculum and noncurriculum classrooms, the question must be raised as to whether the groups were comparable with regard to characteristics such as socioeconomic status, ethnic composition, and general academic skills that may be related to those attributes that were tested. In addition to the question of student comparability, there is the question of teacher comparability. It is known that the curriculum teachers had received training that, since it is part of the curriculum itself, was not in itself an extraneous variable. It is conceivable, however, that the curriculum teachers differed from the noncurriculum teachers in other ways such as general teaching competence, general teaching style, personal characteristics, etc.

2. Loss of subjects: In this study, loss of subjects would be due to simple absence on the testing date for a particular instrument. At this grade level, it seems unlikely that absence would be related to anything systematically affecting the types of measurements that were made. The exception might be that those pupils from the poorest economic strata might have a higher probability of being absent. It is possible for a systematic bias to occur if these absences were higher in either the curriculum or comparison group and if the absent students would score consistently lower or higher.

3. Location selection: A bias could be introduced if more classrooms in one of the two groups (curriculum or comparison) contained features that were conducive to the achievement of the objectives of the curriculum but were not part of the curriculum itself. An example would be school-wide practices favoring independent thinking. The use of two classrooms in a different geographical location could introduce bias if characteristics of the community tended to foster or retard development of curriculum objectives.

4. Extraneous events: The problem here arises from other factors that may have occurred during the course of the year that would affect pupil gains and were unknown to us. Examples would be in-service programs that might affect the teachers' behavior and special events that might affect the students' (e.g., television programming, availability of some of the curriculum

materials, etc.). There is also the possibility of the Hawthorne Effect operating in this kind of study.

5. Maturation: *Because the study was restricted to one
grade level, and the period of time between testings was essentially the same for the two groups, it seems unlikely that there
would be a maturation bias in this study.*

6. Attitude of subjects: *In this study this issue takes
two forms. The first has to do with the attitude of the children with regard to the test taking (pre- and post-). The manner in which they approached the test certainly could affect
their performance. It is possible that children in the curriculum or noncurriculum group might systematically differ in their
attitudes and thus bias the comparisons. The second issue pertains to the teachers and their degree of cooperation in the
study. This is particularly important with regard to the curriculum group since extensive efforts on the part of the teachers are required to adequately implement the curriculum under
study in order to give it a fair test.*

7. Objectivity of data collection: *There is the possibility that individuals doing the testing could differ in their
test administration behavior in such a way as to favor one or
the other of the comparison groups. There is also the problem
that the people scoring the tests, particularly those tests not
completely objective in scoring, might bias the results by knowing which group a particular classroom belonged to.*

8. Effects of sequential measurement: *On some of the
tests, the initial testing might well have a bearing on how
students would respond a second time because the exact same test
was used in both pre- and posttestings. However, because this
factor was constant for both of the groups, it would introduce
no systematic bias.*

9. Instrument decay: *This factor could be a problem if
either the tests themselves or the test administrators were subject to some form of systematic deterioration as a result of repeated testings. An example would be students answering on the
test booklets or defacing them.*

What ways can you think of to handle the problems of possible bias in each category that has been identified by you and
the author?

1. Subject selection: _____

_____

_____

_____

2. Loss of subjects: _____

_____

_____

_____

3. Location of selection: _____

_____

_____

_____

4. Extraneous events: _____

_____

_____

_____

5. Maturation: _____

_____

_____

_____

6. Attitude of subjects: _____

_____

_____

_____

7. Objectivity of data collection: _____

_____

_____

_____

149   Identification of Bias

8.   Effects of sequential measurement (on subjects): _____

_____

_____

_____

9.   Instrument decay: _____

_____

_____

_____

10.   Other: _____

_____

_____

_____

AUTHOR'S COMMENTS

Compare your solutions with what was actually done.
   1.   Subject selection: In order to try to insure comparability of students in the curriculum and noncurriculum groups, each of the noncurriculum classrooms was matched with a curriculum classroom on the basis of socioeconomic status and ethnic composition. Assessment of both of these was made by school district personnel using somewhat crude indices of socioeconomic level and ethnic composition. Nevertheless, we felt considerable confidence that the matching on these variables was quite good with the exception of one classroom in the curriculum group that was comprised of a large number of children of very low socioeconomic status. It was not possible to find a matching classroom of the same degree of economic deprivation in the comparison group. The subsequent finding that the two complete groups of pupils scored very nearly the same on the pretest on the various measures gives additional confidence that the total groups were comparable at the outset with respect to relevant variables.
   With respect to the teachers, those in the noncurriculum group were identified by using a process that was comparable to that used in locating the curriculum teachers for initial involvement with the curriculum. Supervisory personnel in the district were asked to identify teachers who were interested in new developments, who had a high degree of professional identity, and who were sufficiently flexible to be able to accommodate to a new teaching style. Because those were the same criteria that were used to identify teachers for training in the curriculum, it was hoped that this would insure the comparability of the teacher groups on variables mentioned earlier. Subsequent encounters with the teachers in the course of testing supported this judgment with the exception of one or two teachers.
   2.   Loss of subjects: No special provisions were made. Follow-up of absentees would have been desirable, but required more effort and expense than was judged to be warranted.
   3.   Location selection: The only systematic attempt that was made to control this factor was in the procedure for selecting classrooms that matched classrooms on the basis of socioeconomic and ethnic characteristics of pupils. Since these variables are usually found to be related to such variables as adequacy of the physical plant and resources available to teachers and students, some control of these variables was achieved. Further, observations in the classrooms by the investigator suggested that the groups (curriculum and comparison) were comparable with regard to school atmosphere, philosophy, and the like, except for some curriculum schools that exhibited a philosophy more consistent with the curriculum. Thus, bias of this type remains a possibility.

4.   **Extraneous events:** *The principal way of dealing with this issue was to rely on the fact that a number of different schools were involved. It seems unlikely that there would be particular programs or outside events affecting these different schools in such a way as to introduce a systematic bias. It was determined that there were no district-wide programs affecting any of the classrooms that were studied. The possibility of community-wide impact upon the students did remain a possibility.*

5.   **Maturation:** *This factor was controlled by design of the study, i.e., comparisons of curriculum and noncurriculum groups with the same time lapse between pre- and posttesting.*

6.   **Attitude of subjects:** *With regard to student cooperation, the testing was done by people trained by the project staff, all of whom had had previous experience in testing children. A statement was given to all of the classes explaining in a general way the nature of the study and soliciting their cooperation. In addition, each of the testers filled out observation reports on the attitude of the students during testing. For the most part these reports indicated that the attitude of the students in test taking was appropriate. There were, however, a couple of exceptions to this, primarily in the low-income classrooms where the observer reported that some children were not taking the test appropriately. If a bias were introduced in this fashion, it would have worked against the research hypothesis, since this occurred more often in the curriculum classrooms.*

With respect to teacher attitude, all of the curriculum teachers had been involved with the curriculum previously and had expressed a desire to participate in the study. Further, they were provided with several paid in-service days of training in the curriculum. These conditions would all seem to insure that their cooperation was good. Each of the teachers in the curriculum group kept a log of the approximate amount of time spent on the curriculum. The logs indicated considerable variation among the curriculum teachers but indicated that all of them had devoted what was considered to be an adequate amount of time. In addition, all but one of the teachers was observed at least once during the year while conducting a type of discussion that was central to the method. Since these discussions were culminating activities, they added confidence that the preceding activities had also occurred. In addition to this, each of the curriculum classroom teachers made three or four audio-tapes of classroom discussions during the year. These indicators combined with the periodic meetings with the teachers gave additional confidence that the curriculum was in fact being implemented.

With regard to the noncurriculum teachers, the situation was somewhat different. Although they had all agreed to participate in the testing (the extent of participation requested), some expressed dissatisfaction with the time required and with the scheduling of some of the testing. It is possible that this attitude may have been passed on to the students. It seems unlikely, however, that the teachers would have wanted their students to perform poorly on the tests. This does remain as a possible source of bias that would probably work in favor of the curriculum group. Finally, the possibility of a Hawthorne Effect cannot be ruled out because both teachers and students in the curriculum were aware that they were part of a study evaluating a particular curriculum.

7. **Objectivity of data collection:** The testers who did the testing were hired specifically for that purpose and had no vested interest in the way the study came out. Further, in most cases, they were either unaware or unconcerned with which of the comparison groups they happened to be testing. In addition, the prescribed procedures were spelled out in detail to decrease the possibility of such bias intruding. None of the classroom teachers saw copies of any tests until posttesting was completed. In only one class was the teacher present during the testing—in order to facilitate good testing conditions. The judgment was made that teaching for the test would not occur with this teacher, due to her previously demonstrated professional attitude. Results showed that her class did not show an atypical amount of gain in score. With regard to scoring, most tests were machine scored. For those requiring judging of answers, the classrooms were coded by members of the research team and the code was unknown to the person doing the actual scoring so that the possibility of scoring bias was eliminated.

8. **Effects of sequential measurement:** This was controlled by the research design that made it constant for the two groups.

9. **Instrument decay:** The test booklets were examined and any with marks on them were thrown out. The tests were not used so extensively as to be subject to much deterioration, nor did the testers work so exhaustively as to make it likely that their performance was affected.

Next, examine your proposed study for possible sources of bias. Try to identify problems and possible ways to handle them in each category. Some adjustment of your procedures, as you described them previously, will probably be necessary.

1. Subject selection: Problem: _____

_____

_____

_____

153 Identification of Bias

Solution: _____

_____

_____

_____

2. Loss of subjects: Problem: _____

_____

_____

_____

Solution: _____

_____

_____

_____

3. Location selection: Problem: _____

_____

_____

_____

Solution: _____

_____

_____

_____

4. Extraneous events: Problem: _____

_____

_____

_____

Solution: _____

_____

_____

_____

5. Maturation: Problem: _____

_____

_____

_____

Solution: _____

_____

_____

_____

6. Attitude of subjects: Problem: _____

_____

_____

_____

Solution: _____

_____

_____

_____

7. Objectivity of data collection: Problem: _____

_____

_____

_____

Solution: _____

_____

_____

_____

8.   Effects of sequential measurement (on subjects): Problem: _____

_____

_____

_____

Solution: _____

_____

_____

_____

9.   Instrument decay: Problem: _____

_____

_____

_____

Solution: _____

_____

_____

_____

10.   Other: Problem: _____

_____

_____

_____

Solution: _____

_____

_____

_____

   The procedure as you have planned it to this point may not
be feasible within the amount of time you can allot to this
course. It should be feasible, however, to do at least a pilot
study. This requires that you try out as much of your procedure
as possible, making adjustments where necessary. Plan to use at
least one of your instruments to gather data on at least ten to
twenty subjects. This will give you firsthand experience in
data collection. In the next chapter we will examine methods
for making sense out of data. You will be able to use some of
these methods with your own data. The more data you have, the
more meaningful this experience will be. A pilot study is done
to get feedback on how procedures and instruments work and to
get some preliminary data. Because it usually lacks the rigor
of the real study, one can seldom make much of the results.
   Describe in detail the procedures you will follow in your
pilot study. Try to carry it out as soon as possible. You will
be asked to report on your pilot study in chapter six.

   Procedures for pilot study: _____

_____

_____

_____

_____

_____

_____

_____

_____

_____

_____

SUMMARY

This chapter has dealt with the major ways in which a study can be misleading (contaminated, biased). Some techniques for identifying and eliminating defects in order to get a legitimate test of the research hypothesis have been discussed.

Now that you have considered possible sources of bias in your study, you may want to revise other parts of your plan. Perhaps you will select subjects differently or decide to use different instruments. If so, make the necessary revisions in the appropriate sections of the book.

You should be aware that a number of more specific research designs have been developed as ways of handling certain kinds of bias. A good reference is the Campbell and Stanley citation below.

The next chapter deals with ways of simplifying data in order to make it comprehensible. If you are fearful of statistics, you may be interested in knowing that one of the best selling texts in statistics was written by a man who had great difficulty in his own statistical course work.

Major concepts considered in this chapter were:

Procedures	Experimentation
Single group design	Matching
Multiple group design	Procedural bias
Variable	Sources of bias
Contamination	
Extraneous variable	

REFERENCES FOR FURTHER READING

Campbell, D. T., and Stanley, J. C. "Experimental and Quasi-Experimental Designs for Research on Teaching." In N. L. Gage, ed., *Handbook of Research on Teaching*. Chicago: Rand McNally, 1963.

Englehart, M. *Methods of Educational Research*. Chicago: Rand McNally, 1972. Chap. 12.

Good, C. V. *Essentials of Educational Research*. New York, N.Y.: Appleton-Century-Crofts, 1959. Chap. 8.

Helmstadter, G. C. *Researcher Concepts in Human Behavior*. New York, N.Y.: Appleton-Century-Crofts, 1970. Chap. 4.

Kerlinger, F. M. *Foundations of Behavioral Research*. New York, N.Y.: Holt, Rinehart & Winston, 1964. Chaps. 15-22.

Levine, S., and Elzey, F. F. *A Programmed Introduction to Research*. Belmont, Calif.: Wadsworth, 1968. Chap. 4.

Data Analysis
or "How to Make Sense Out of Information"

INTRODUCTION

On completing this chapter you should be able to identify the most common techniques for analyzing data and where their use is appropriate. You will have decided on techniques to use in your proposed study and will apply them to your pilot study data. You should also be able to interpret the common forms of statistical tables.

Once information has been obtained through use of the research instruments (interviews, ratings, tests, etc.), one needs to make sense out of it. How is the information to be used to answer the research question or test the research hypothesis? Statistical procedures are of great help at this point. They enable us to organize and simplify information. In this chapter, previously mentioned studies will be used to provide examples of the most commonly used statistical techniques.

SINGLE GROUP DESIGNS

Chapter four discussed two basic research designs: the single group and the multiple group designs. In the single group design, the relationship between two variables is studied. The open classroom study is an example of this design and provides an opportunity to illustrate how raw data can be put in a form that is interpretable. The raw data from this study are presented in table 5.1.

What can you tell about the relationship between openness and motivation from studying table 5.1 (on page 161)?

Scatterplot. In order to clarify the relationship between openness and motivation, it is useful to make a scatterplot. To do so, each classroom must be plotted as on page 112.

Suppose we made a scatterplot and it turned out as figure 5.1.

FIGURE 5.1

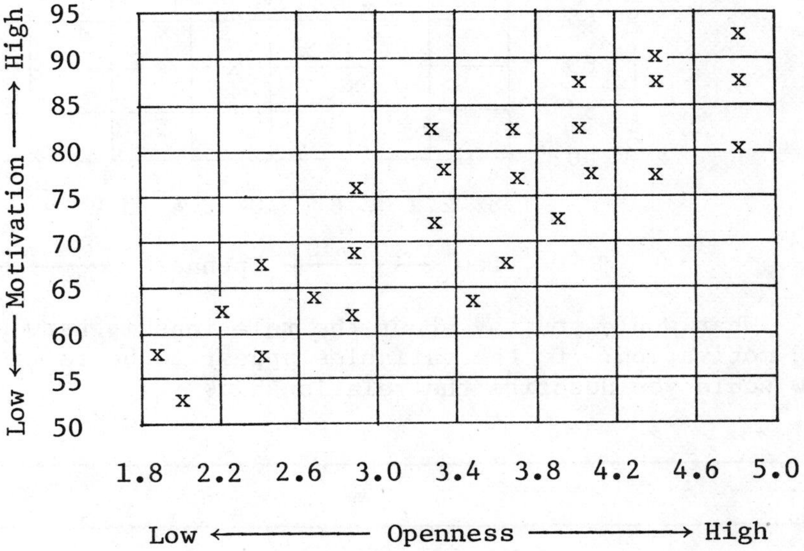

What would you say about the relationship between openness and motivation? Do the variables appear to be related? If so, how would you describe the relationship?

Now suppose it turned out instead to look like figure 5.2.

FIGURE 5.2

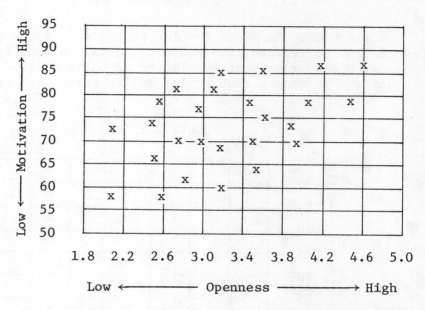

What would you say about the relationship between openness and motivation? Do the variables appear to be related? If so, how would you describe the relationship?

_____

_____

Next, make the actual scatterplot from the table 5.1 data by entering each classroom in figure 5.3 (pages 162 and 163). Classrooms 1 and 2 have been done; your task is to enter the remaining classrooms. If you need help in making the scatterplot, refer to page 112.

This one is harder to interpret than the ones before. What can you say about the relationship between openness and motivation based on the scatterplot? Do the variables appear to be related? If so, how would you describe the relationship? _____

_____

_____

_____

_____

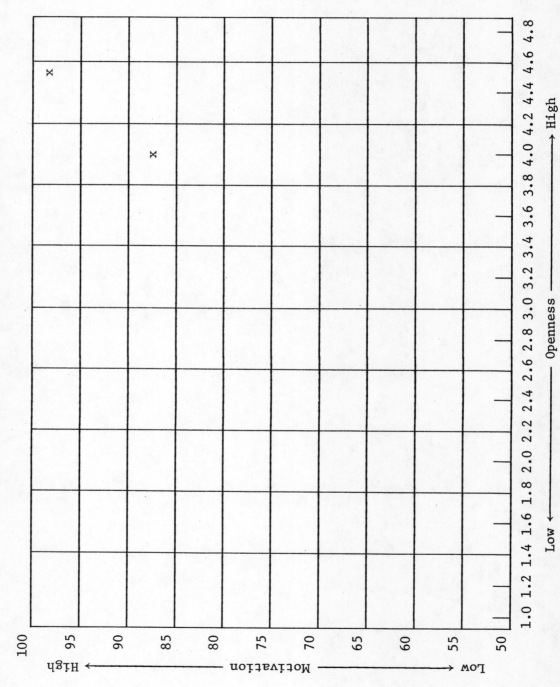

FIGURE 5.3
SCATTERPLOT SHOWING RELATIONSHIP BETWEEN
OPENNESS AND MOTIVATION FOR TWENTY-SIX CLASSROOMS

TABLE 5.1
RAW DATA ON OPENNESS AND MOTIVATION FOR
TWENTY-SIX CLASSROOMS

Classroom	Openness Rating	Motivation (% Attenders)
1	4.5	97
2	4.0	88
3	2.4	77
4	1.9	64
5	1.8	67
6	4.7	91
7	1.7	82
8	1.9	89
9	4.1	99
10	4.2	67
11	4.1	83
12	4.2	94
13	4.4	85
14	4.7	84
15	3.4	93
16	3.2	90
17	3.3	86
18	4.4	73
19	3.4	74
20	1.9	70
21	4.6	85
22	3.1	96
23	5.7	54
24	4.5	90
25	3.7	82
26	4.0	75

AUTHOR'S COMMENTS

It is very difficult to tell what relationship exists from looking only at table 5.1. Once the scatterplot has been made, however, the relationship becomes clear. Figure 5.1 would indicate a strong relationship because classrooms rated high in openness scored high in motivation. Classrooms rated lower in openness scored lower in motivation. Figure 5.2 would indicate a much lower relationship. The fact that there are no classrooms in the upper left and lower right portions indicates some relationship. Figure 5.3 (the actual data) shows that there is very little relationship between openness and motivation for these classrooms. There is a slight tendency for classrooms at the high end of the openness scale to also be high on the motivation scale, but it is not very pronounced; there are several classrooms that are high on openness but low on motivation. Similarly, classrooms rated low in openness cover a wide range of motivation scores. (Keep in mind the many limitations of this study that were discussed previously. You will recall that these reasons included lack of representativeness of the sample and poor reliability and validity of the measures due to using only one observation period. Consequently, these data do not provide an adequate test of the research hypothesis.) Figure 5.3 also shows that there are two distinct groupings of classrooms on degree of openness. Six rooms cluster at the low end with the remainder at the high end of the openness variable. As it happens, these groups correspond to the original designation of the classrooms by reputation. This would provide evidence of the validity of openness ratings except that most observers had knowledge of the classrooms reputation before observing (a possible source of bias that was discussed in chapter four). Figure 5.3 also suggests that there are greater differences in degree of motivation in classrooms rated more open than in those rated less open. This interpretation is very tentative due to the small sample size.

What in figure 5.3 suggests that there are greater differences in degree of motivation in classrooms rated more open than in those rated less open?

_____

_____

_____

Correlation Coefficient. As we have seen, the scatterplot is one means of clarifying the relationship between two variables for a particular group. A second means of doing so is through the use of a numerical index called the *correlation coefficient*. This is simply *a number* that represents the degree of relationship (correlation) between two variables for a particular group. It is useful because it is a convenient way of representing relationships, particularly if one wishes to describe a great many relationships in the same study.

The starting point for obtaining a correlation coefficient is exactly the same as for a scatterplot. That is, one must have a measurement of both variables for each unit being studied. Thus, in the open classroom study, we had a measure of openness and a measure of motivation for each classroom. In studies in which the person is the unit being measured, one would have to have a measure for both variables for each person in the sample. One then carries out a series of computations that result in a number called the correlation coefficient. The computations are not difficult, but they are most appropriately treated in a course on statistics.

For present purposes, it is important that you understand how to interpret a correlation coefficient. Correlation coefficients can take on any values between −1.00 and +1.00 and are usually reported to two decimal places. A value of .00 represents a complete absence of any relationship. The maximum possible relationship is 1.00; it indicates that one of the variables increases in degree as the other increases. A value of −1.00 indicates the same *amount* of relationship as 1.00, but the minus sign indicates that as one variable *increases* in amount, the other *decreases*. We would, for example, expect a negative correlation (if any) between bowling average and golf average because the more skillful person will have a high bowling average but a low golf average (since a good performance in golf receives a low score whereas a good performance in bowling receives a high score).

The most commonly used symbol for the correlation coefficient is the lower case r. Thus, the verbal statement that a correlation coefficient was computed to be .52 is symbolically expressed as r = .52. Correlations as high as .90 are customarily encountered only when correlating one form of a test with an alternate form. This is the basis for determining the reliability of measurements. Thus, one of the uses of the correlation coefficient is to describe the reliability of measurements. In this usage, of course, one would hope to have a very high positive correlation between two forms of a test or between two administrations of the same test. When investigating the relationship between two *different* variables, it is unusual to find correlations much higher than .70 in the behavioral sciences.

If you will study the scatterplots in figure 5.4 and the accompanying correlation coefficient for each, you will acquire an understanding of the degree of relationship indicated by differing numerical values of the correlation coefficient.

It may help to think in terms of predicting one variable from the other. Let the arrows in each picture represent the scores for two persons (A and B) on the horizontal axis. Assume we do not have their scores on the other variable[1] (i.e., on the vertical axis). We could in each picture predict what their scores on the other variables would probably be. To do this, first draw an ellipse around those points that are within a narrow band directly above A. Notice that these points represent individuals whose scores on the horizontal axis were all very close to A. Next examine the scores on the vertical axis for these same points (individuals). Take an approximate average of those scores and represent it by an arrow drawn to the vertical axis. This is portrayed on the first two scatterplots. If you will follow this procedure for each of the plots, you will, I think, observe two things:

a) The higher the numerical value of the correlation coefficient (whether + or -), the further apart are the predicted scores for the two individuals (whose scores on the horizontal axis remain the same throughout).

b) The higher the correlation coefficient (whether + or -), the more closely grouped are the scores to be averaged.

This means that the higher the correlation, the better predictions we can make—which is another way of saying that the variables are more highly related.

Notice that with positive correlations, person B is always predicted to score higher on the vertical axis than person A. With negative correlations, person B is always predicted to score lower.

After studying these scatterplots, indicate your estimate of the correlation coefficient that would be obtained for the two scatterplots that you have examined previously.

Estimate of correlation coefficient on page 112: _____

Estimate of correlation coefficient on page 162: _____ [2]

---

[1] It makes no difference, for this purpose, what the variables are. If you wish, label the graphs (e.g., the vertical axis could represent weight; the horizontal could represent height).

[2] See page 204 for answers.

FIGURE 5.4
SCATTERPLOTS AND CORRELATION COEFFICIENTS SHOWING
DIFFERENT DEGREES OF RELATIONSHIP
(Letters represent hypothetical individuals.)

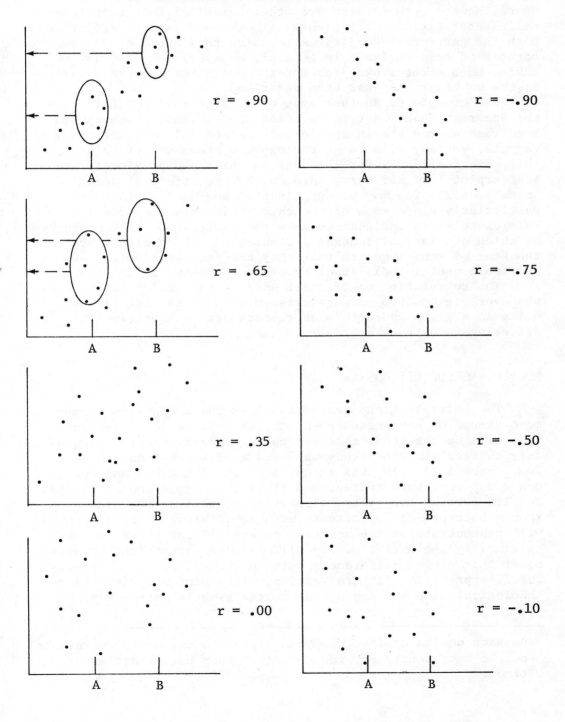

The discussion up to this point regarding the correlation coefficient has applied to what is technically called the Pearson Product-Moment Correlation Coefficient, which is probably the most widely used correlation coefficient. You should be aware, however, that there are other numerical indices that are called correlation coefficients. These correlations differ in both the particular conditions to which they apply and in the methods of computation. In general, however, you will not be making much error if you interpret these other numerical indices in the way that has just been described.

One example of another type of correlation coefficient is the Spearman Rank Order Correlation Coefficient, which can be used when scores are in rank order. Since this is quite easy to compute, you may wish to go through the procedure of calculating this numerical index for the data on which you previously made a scatterplot. If so, carry through the operations as described in table 5.2. You may be surprised at how easy it is to do, particularly since much of the calculating has been done for you. This exercise is included to take the mystery out of the process by which statistical indexes are obtained, to partially overcome the fear of many students that they can't do statistics, and to provide a useful tool, should you have occasion to use it.

The correlation coefficient and/or scatterplot may be used whenever one has two measurements on each of the individual units in a group and both measurements are quantitative (take on differing amounts or degrees).

MULTIPLE GROUP DESIGNS

The multiple group design involves the comparison of two or more groups on some measurement.[3]   Our vehicle for illustration here will be the study that evaluated a social studies elementary curriculum. The study was used as Example 2 in chapter four (page 142). In this study, a curriculum group and comparison group were both tested, and it is the comparison of the test results for the two groups with which we will be concerned. Although both pre- and posttests were administered, our discussion will concentrate on the posttest or end-of-year scores in order to simplify the analysis. We will examine a test (one of many used) that showed differences between the groups. This test, the Interpretation of Data Test, provided students with an archaelogical site map and a code to the symbols on the map.

---

[3]The same design applies when one wishes to compare measurements on the *same* instrument for the *same* group but at different times.

Then twenty-six multiple-choice questions were asked involving
map reading, making inferences about the use of objects, making
inferences about how objects influenced each other at the site,
making generalizations about the site based on all the data, and
asking what other kinds of information would be needed for particular generalizations. The study was done to see how the
curriculum and comparison groups performed on this test and hypothesized that the curriculum group would score higher. The
number of cases was 227 in the curriculum group and 260 in the
comparison group. Clearly, visual inspection of this number of
scores would provide very little understanding of how the groups
compared.

Frequency Polygon. One convenient way to clarify such
data is by drawing a picture of the results in the form of a
frequency polygon. A frequency polygon is made by plotting the
number (or percentage) of individuals falling within certain
score intervals and connecting the points. Figure 5.5 shows a
frequency polygon for each of the two groups in the curriculum
study. It shows, for example, that a score of 18 was attained
by 3 percent of the comparison group and 5 percent of the curriculum group.

FIGURE 5.5
FREQUENCY POLYGONS FOR CURRICULUM AND
COMPARISON GROUPS FOR INTERPRETATION OF DATA TEST

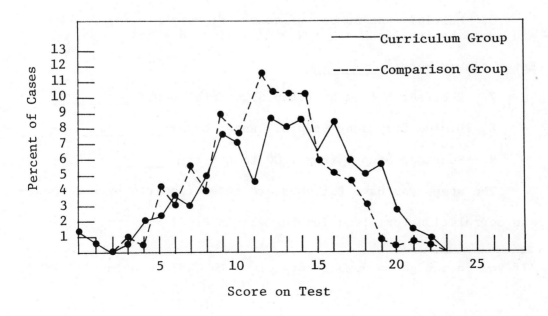

/////////////////////// OPTIONAL EXERCISE ///////////////////////

TABLE 5.2
COMPUTING THE SPEARMAN RANK ORDER CORRELATION COEFFICIENT

1. For each variable, rank the scores from high to low. In case of ties, give the average rank to each. All rankings have been done for classroom openness. Notice that there are three 4.7's, which is the highest score. These use up ranks 1, 2, and 3; so each gets the average rank of 2.0. The 4.6 uses up rank 4. The two 4.5's use up ranks 5 and 6, so each gets 5.5. Study the rankings that have been done and then rank the remaining classrooms on motivation.

2. The hard part is done. Notice that Step 1 is much easier if the data are ranks to start with (they often are). Next, take the difference in ranks for each room and enter it in the D column. D equals openness rank minus motivation rank. This has been done for most rooms.

3. Multiply each D by itself (square it). Enter in the D^2 column. (For *this* practice exercise *only*, you may drop the decimals before squaring, i.e., 9.5 becomes 9.0; $9.0^2 = 81$. Remember, $-3^2 = +9$.)

4. Total the D^2 column; enter here: _____

5. Multiply Step 4 by 6; enter here: _____

6. Multiply the number of cases (N; here N = 26) by itself and again by itself: $N \times N \times N = N^3 = 26 \times 26 \times 26$.

Enter answer here: _____

7. Subtract N from N^3 (Step 5). Enter here: _____

8. Divide Step 5 by Step 6. Enter here: _____

9. Subtract Step 8 from 1.00 to get r = _____ [4]

The steps you have followed are those required by the Spearman correlation formula. The formula is $r = 1 - \dfrac{6 \Sigma D^2}{N^3 - N}$

---

[4]If you do not get a number very close to .23, recheck your work.

Classroom Number	Openness Score	Openness Rank	Motivation Score	Motivation Rank	D	D^2
1	4.5	5.5	97	2.0	3.5	9
2	4.0	13.5	88	10.0	3.5	9
3	2.4	21.0	77			
4	1.9	23.0	64			
5	1.8	25.0	67			
6	4.7	2.0	91	6.0	-4.0	16
7	1.7	26.0	82	16.5	9.5	81
8	1.9	23.0	89	9.0	14.0	196
9	4.1	11.5	99	1.0	10.5	100
10	4.2	9.5	67			
11	4.1	11.5	83	15.0	-3.5	9
12	4.2	9.5	94	4.0	5.5	25
13	4.4	7.5	85	12.5	-5.0	25
14	4.7	2.0	84	14.0	-12.0	144
15	3.4	16.5	93	5.0	11.5	121
16	3.2	19.0	90	7.5	11.5	121
17	3.3	18.0	86	11.0	7.0	49
18	4.4	7.5	73			
19	3.4	16.5	74			
20	1.9	23.0	70			
21	4.6	4.0	85	12.5	-8.5	64
22	3.1	20.0	96	3.0	17.0	289
23	4.7	2.0	54			
24	4.5	5.5	90	7.5	-2.0	4
25	3.7	15.0	82	16.5	-1.5	1
26	4.0	13.5	75			

$$\Sigma \ D^2 \ =$$

How do the groups compare? Was the hypothesis supported?

_____

_____

_____

_____

_____

AUTHOR'S COMMENTS

Figure 5.5 indicates that on this test the curriculum group did perform at a higher level than the comparison group. There is little difference between the two polygons at the lower end of the scale. However, the comparison group contains a substantially higher percentage of cases in the middle range of the test, whereas the curriculum group has a substantially larger proportion scoring at the higher end of the test.

Averages. In a multiple group design, it is often helpful to use a single numerical index for each group. You are already familiar with the use of the average (more technically the arithmetic mean), which is obtained by adding all of the scores and dividing by the number of cases. (An example of this procedure occurred on page 113.) A second index that is frequently used is called the median. It is the *point* in a distribution below which 50 percent of the cases fall.[5] In figure 5.5, estimate the median for each of the two groups by looking at the graph. Remember that it is the *point* that will have half of the cases or half of the area above and below it.

Estimated median for curriculum group: _____

Estimated median for comparison group: _____ [6]

The frequency polygon, the median, and the average or arithmetic mean may be used whenever one is comparing two or more distinct groups on a measure that is quantitative (i.e., takes on differing degrees or amounts).

Crossbreaks. In the preceding technique, at least one of the variables being studied was quantitative. That is, it could be meaningfully considered to take on differing amounts or degrees.[7] However, not all variables are quantitative. Some are qualitative, meaning that they differ in kind but *not* in amount or degree. When studying the relationship between two *qualitative* variables, a technique called the *crossbreak* provides a convenient way of clarifying information. The categories for

---

[5] If the number of cases is even, the median is the point midway between the two middle scores.

[6] See page 204 for answers.

[7] Recall definition in note 1 on p. 111.

each variable are specified and individuals tallied where they
fit the intersection of categories. As an example, suppose that
one wished to study the relationship between type of therapeutic
approach used by counselors and the institution from which the
counselor's training was obtained. Both the institution variable and the type of therapy variable would constitute qualitative variables because the categories within them could differ,
but not in *amount*. This relationship can be studied by means
of a crossbreak table such as table 5.3. Each individual is
tallied in one (and only one) cell that corresponds to the combination of his therapeutic approach and institution. The total
frequency (number of tallies) is recorded for each cell.

This table indicates that Happy Valley State emphasized
Gestalt, Multiversity II primarily emphasized Behavior Modification, and College of the Specific produced more Rogerian thera-
pists.

TABLE 5.3
EXAMPLE OF CROSSBREAK TABLE: COMPARISON OF
THERAPEUTIC METHOD AND TRAINING INSTITUTION
(Fictitious data.)

| Training Institution | Therapeutic Method | | | |
	Rogerian	Gestalt	Behavior Modification	Freudian
Happy Valley State	7	20	10	8
Multiversity II	8	6	25	11
College of the Specific	15	10	5	5

Crossbreak tables (sometimes called contingency tables) are
used whenever both variables are qualitative. Crossbreaks are
also often used when one variable is qualitative and the other
is quantitative. You will recall that this was the condition
under which we previously used the frequency polygon and comparison of means or medians. When the variable that differs in
amount (is quantitative) lends itself easily to numerical description—as in the case of test scores, ratings, and the like
—one usually compares averages. When, however, it is not clear
how the numbers should be assigned to different categories, the
data can be treated through crossbreaks.

Examples of crossbreaks are shown in table 5.4 with data
taken from the evaluation study of the inner-city school discussed in chapters three and four. The questions studied were,
"How are different components of the project perceived?" and,
"Do different staff groups perceive a given component differently?" Table 5.4 presents two components of the program,
using crossbreak tables. The first component is the "use of

paraprofessionals in the school," and the second is the "degree
of cooperation among teachers." The interview data that formed
the basic information were first categorized within three groups
of respondents: teachers; paraprofessionals; and the remaining
staff (primarily administration since several cafeteria and custodial staff members said they could not evaluate these particular components). Since each individual had rated each component
as excellent, good, fair, or poor, each individual response
could be tallied within one category. For example, there were
seven teachers who said that the paraprofessional aspect of the
program was good. In this case the three groups of respondents
constitute a variable that is clearly qualitative. The ratings
of poor to excellent could be assigned numerical values and the
average computed for each of the three groups. It is not clear,
however, whether the assignment of numbers to these categories
should be, in order, 1, 2, 3, 4 or perhaps 1, 2, 4, 6. In this
instance it was decided instead to treat the data as qualitative.

TABLE 5.4
RATINGS OF TWO PROGRAM COMPONENTS BY THREE SCHOOL GROUPS

Program Component and Rating Group	Rating				
	Excellent	Good	Fair	Poor	Total
a) Paraprofessionals:					
Teachers	17	7	5	0	29
Paraprofessionals	12	15	1	0	28
Other Staff	6	6	2	0	14
Total	35	28	8	0	71
b) Cooperation Among Teachers:					
Teachers	5	7	12	6	30
Paraprofessionals	6	12	7	3	28
Other Staff	2	3	4	5	14
Total	13	22	23	14	72

Study table 5.4 and analyze each program component in terms
of a relationship between rating group and rating given.

Table 5.4-a _____

_____

_____

Table 5.4-b _____

_____

_____

AUTHOR'S COMMENTS

Table 5.4-a shows that teachers rated paraprofessionals somewhat higher than did paraprofessionals themselves or other staff, although the preponderance of all ratings is in the excellent and good categories.

Table 5.4-b shows that paraprofessionals rated cooperation among teachers slightly more positively than did the teachers themselves or other staff.

Table 5.5 summarizes the preceding statistical procedures and when they are used. To use table 5.5 you must decide whether a particular study is a single group or multiple group design and whether each variable is to be considered as quantitative or qualitative. Having done so, the table tells which techniques are appropriate.

TABLE 5.5
SUMMARY OF BASIC DESCRIPTIVE STATISTICS

Conditions	Procedure
When studying the relationship between two variables for one group of subjects *and both* variables are *quantitative*, i.e., take on the property of amount or degree	Scatterplot and/or correlation coefficient
When studying the relationship between two variables for one group of subjects *and both* variables are *qualitative*, i.e., are described by categories that do not differ in amount or degree	Crossbreak table
When comparing *two or more* groups of subjects on a measurement that is considered to be *quantitative*	Frequency polygon and/or median or mean
When comparing *two or more* groups of subjects on a measurement that is considered to be *qualitative*	Crossbreak table

Note: The researcher sometimes must make a judgment as to whether a measurement is most meaningfully considered as quantitative or qualitative.

For each of the following examples, write the statistical procedure that you would use to clarify the data. Also make a diagram showing how the results might look. Use the figures in this chapter as models. In some cases, more than one procedure may be appropriate.

1. Comparing students in special classes with similar students not in special classes as to scores on a self-concept test:

2. Relating the number of positive counselor comments contained in audio-tapes of interviews to changes in counselee scores over a three-month period on a test of ego strength:

3.   Comparing answers of a group of fifth-graders to these two questions: How do you feel about your teacher? And do most of the kids in the room like their classmates? Each student's response to each question is classified as generally positive, neutral, generally negative, or indeteriminate:

4.   Relating the score on the odd-numbered items of the Q-E Intelligence Test (see page 61) to the score on the even-numbered items for a group of college students:

5. Relating teacher scores on the Picture Situation Inventory Control Score to the number of controlling statements made over several observation periods as judged by observers (see page 74):

6. Relating teacher scores on the Picture Situation Inventory Communication Score to administrator ratings of teacher effectiveness as below average, average, or above average (see page 75):

7.   Comparing teacher perceptions of the effectiveness of
the use of paraprofessionals with their perception of the degree
of cooperation among teachers in a particular school (see table
5.4, page 176):

8.   Comparing first-, second-, and third-graders' answers
to interview questions as to how much they liked school. Each
answer is categorized as very much, some, a little, or not much:

9. Comparing the score on the AGT test obtained from the number of correct answers with the score obtained from categorization of the interview answers (see page 67):

10. Relating scores on the Picture Situation Inventory Control Score to the observer rating of the amount of noise in the classroom on a 5-point scale:

AUTHOR'S COMMENTS

The appropriate procedures are as follows:
Example 1.   Frequency polygon and/or mean or median (two
            groups compared on a quantitative variable)
Example 2.   Correlation coefficient and/or scatterplot
            (one group, both variables quantitative)
Example 3.   Crossbreak table (one group, both variables
            best treated as qualitative; if "indeterminate"
            is deleted, correlation could be used)
Example 4.   Correlation coefficient and/or scatterplot
            (one group, both measures quantitative)
Example 5.   Correlation coefficient and/or scatterplot
            (one group, both measures quantitative)
Example 6.   a) (one group) If administrative ratings
               treated as quantitative and assigned num-
               bers, correlation coefficient and/or
               scatterplot
            b) If administrative ratings treated as quali-
               tative, test scores also grouped in cate-
               gories; crossbreak tables, e.g.:

| | | Ratings | |
		Below Average	Average	Above Average
	High	_____	_____	_____
Test Scores	Medium	_____	_____	_____
	Low	_____	_____	_____

Example 7.   Crossbreak table (one group, both variables
            treated as qualitative; correlation could be
            used if both variables considered quantitative)
Example 8.   a) (three groups) If numbers assigned to cate-
               gories of "liking," frequency distribution
               and/or mean or median for each group
            b) If categories treated as qualitative, cross-
               break table, e.g.:

	Ratings			
	Very Much	Some Liking	Little Liking	Not Much Liking
Grade Level 3	_____	_____	_____	_____
2	_____	_____	_____	_____
1	_____	_____	_____	_____

Example 9. Correlation coefficient and/or scatterplot (one group, both variables quantitative)

Example 10. Same as example 6 (depends on whether ratings treated as quantitative or qualitative; probably the former; note that relationship is negative)

Describe below the statistical procedures you think would be appropriate to use in *your* proposed study and give an illustration of how the data might appear. Hopefully, you will collect enough data in your pilot study to try these procedures.

What procedure(s) will you use? _____

_____

Why will you use this (these) procedure(s)? _____

_____

_____

_____

Show a sketch or diagram of how the results might look.

STATISTICAL INFERENCE

In the preceding part of this chapter you became acquainted with the more commonly used techniques for making sense out of information, or more precisely, for describing relationships in research data. Note that in all the examples given in the preceding sections, the relationship was *described* as it occurred in the data collected on a specified *sample*.

The next issue to consider is closely related to the topic of sampling discussed in chapter three. It deals with the question of generalizing a relationship found in a particular sample to a broader group, i.e., a population. If a substantial relationship has been demonstrated within the sample studied, as, for example, by means of crossbreaks or a correlation coefficient, one will probably want to generalize the finding to the population. However, one cannot expect, even if one studies the entire population, to find precisely the same relationship that was found for the particular sample. Considered another way, if one were to take a second sample in precisely the same fashion, one would expect to find results that would be similar but not precisely the same as were found in the first sample because different people would be included. Under certain conditions, precise mathematical procedures have been devised for estimating the degree to which the statistic obtained (e.g., a correlation coefficient) would differ between the sample and the population. These procedures assume that the sample has been drawn randomly from the population.

When attempting to generalize a sample finding to the population, the particular question most often asked is, "Is it likely that a relationship as large as that obtained for the *sample* could have happened if there is no relationship at all in the *population*?" It is easy to think of examples where this would be likely. Suppose, for example, that we were interested in the relationship between performance on an algebra test and length of index finger for the population of all high school seniors. We might, if we used a sample of five or ten students selected randomly, discover some such relationship (perhaps a correlation coefficient of .60), even though we would probably obtain a correlation of .00 if we were to study the entire population. The use of very small samples is thus likely to produce a relationship that is due to nothing more than chance, i.e., to characteristics of the particular individuals who happened to be selected for the sample.

The next question to be asked, therefore, is, "What is the probability of obtaining a relationship as large as the one in the sample, if in fact there is no relationship at all in the population?" By *probability*, we simply mean the odds. For example, what are the odds of obtaining a correlation as large as

.60 with a sample of five cases if, in fact, there is no relationship (.00 correlation) in the population? The odds or
chances may be one in two or one in three or one in ten or one
in fifty or one in ten thousand or some other value. If we can
assess the odds (the probability) of this happening, we are in a
much better position to judge whether or not there is any basis
for generalizing our sample findings to the population. The
purpose of statistical inference is to provide this probability.

The logic and mathematics involved in developing techniques
for this purpose are beyond the scope of this book. However, if
you do the optional exercise on page 188 you will, I think, gain
some insight into the general approach. In any case, our objective is for you to become sufficiently familiar with the process
so that you can (a) select an appropriate technique for getting
the probability, and (b) interpret the probability.

For an illustration, we shall use the results from the open
classroom study. You will recall that we computed a correlation
coefficient of .23 between classroom openness and student motivation. Even though this represents a rather slight relationship, we may wish to determine the probability of its occurrence
if there is really no relationship ($r = .00$) in the population.
In this case the appropriate technique is called the 't' *test*.
You can calculate the numerical value of 't' for this example by
doing the optional exercise on page 190. Having calculated this
numerical index ($t = 1.15$), we can translate it into a probability by using a mathematical table (usually labeled "Probabilities for the 't' distribution") found in most statistics
texts. Reading such a table gives us $p = .15$, which tells us
that the probability of obtaining a correlation as large or
larger than .23 by chance when there is *no* relationship in the
population is 15 out of 100.

,,,,,,,,,,,,,,,,,,,,, Optional Exercise ,,,,,,,,,,,,,,,,,,,,,

TABLE 5.6
SAMPLING DISTRIBUTION

Take a coin and test the hypothesis that the coin is dishonest, i.e., it gives more heads than tails.

Procedure: Flip the coin four times. Record the number of heads here: _____

Based on this amount of data, would you accept or reject the hypothesis? _____ Why? _____

_____

Suppose you had gotten four heads (maybe you did). Would you accept or reject the hypothesis? _____ Why? _____

_____

Flip the same coin four more times and record the number of heads. Note: Each set of four flips will be considered a *sample*. For each sample the possible number of heads is: 0, 1, 2, 3, or 4. Repeat and enter for a total of sixteen samples (four flips each).

Sample Number	Number of Heads	Sample Number	Number of Heads
1	_____	9	_____
2	_____	10	_____
3	_____	11	_____
4	_____	12	_____
5	_____	13	_____
6	_____	14	_____
7	_____	15	_____
8	_____	16	_____

Next tally the number of times each possible outcome occurred. Then change each to a percent by dividing each by 16.

Outcome	Number of Times	Percent
0 heads	_____	_____
1 head	_____	_____
2 heads	_____	_____
3 heads	_____	_____
4 heads	_____	_____

If you were to use several coins and many more samples you
would (almost certainly) arrive at a table that presents the results to be expected with an honest coin.

Outcome	Percent	Probablity
0 heads	6	.06
1 head	25	.25
2 heads	38	.38
3 heads	25	.25
4 heads	6	.06
Total	100	1.00

These percentages are actually probabilities. They tell us
how often we would expect each outcome to occur with an honest
coin.

Next, return to your original sample (the first set of four

flips) for the coin in question. Is your interpretation of re-

sults any different? _____ What would be your interpretation

if the results of that sample had been four heads? _____

What if the results had been three heads? _____

//

AUTHOR'S COMMENTS

Since the probability of getting four heads on any given sample is only .06, this outcome for the first sample would lead me to tentatively accept the hypothesis that the coin is dishonest. Any other outcome would clearly not support the hypothesis.

The procedure just followed is essentially that used in deriving probabilities in any statistical inference technique. That is, the outcome from a particular sample is compared to a distribution of possible outcomes and its probability determined. The details, however, are considerably more complex.

\`\`\`\`\`\`\`\`\`\`\`\`\`\`\`\`\`\`\`\`\`\`\` Optional Exercise \`\`\`\`\`\`\`\`\`\`\`\`\`\`\`\`\`\`\`\`\`\`\`

TABLE 5.7
CALCULATING 't' TEST FOR DIFFERENCE BETWEEN MEANS

1.   Subtract 2 from the number of cases (26) = _____

2.   Take square root of Step 1   = _____

3.   Multiply Step 2 by r (= .23)   = _____

4.   Square r   = _____

5.   Subtract Step 4 from 1   = _____

6.   Take square root of Step 5   = _____

7.   Divide Step 3 by Step 6 to get t   = _____ [8]

The steps you have followed are expressed
by the formula:

$$t_r = \frac{r\sqrt{N-2}}{\sqrt{1-r^2}}$$

In practice, there are certain probabilities that are taken as indicative of a stable nonchance relationship. If the probability of obtaining the degree of relationship shown in our sample is less than .05 (one chance in 20), it is customary to take it as *statistically significant* or probably *not* due to chance. Clearly, if the probability is less than 5 percent (for example, 1 percent), we can be more confident that we are not simply dealing with chance. These values (1 percent and 5 percent) are frequently spoken of as levels of significance.

---

[8]You should get a result very near t = 1.15.

Consequently, when a report states that a particular relationship was significant at the 5 percent level, it means that the
chances of the finding being simply a fluke, due to the particular sample that was used, are less than 5 in 100. It means that
the relationship is worth noting and is tentatively acceptable as
a reproducible relationship for a specified population. Note
that statistical significance is not the same as practical significance. A correlation of .23 can, under certain circumstances, be statistically significant. It is, however, too low
to be of practical use in most circumstances.

   Determining Statistical Significance. There are techniques
appropriate for use with each of the descriptive statistics discussed earlier in this chapter. The most common are summarized
in table 5.8. This table may be used in two ways. First, given
a particular condition or way of describing a relationship, the
table shows one or more techniques that may be used to determine
statistical significance. Thus, if one wishes to test whether
a difference in two means is greater than chance and the number
in each group is greater than 30, either a 't' test or critical
ratio may be used. Once one has selected an appropriate procedure, the choice is to learn how to carry out the analysis or
find someone who knows how.
   The second purpose served by table 5.8 is to make interpretation of published tables meaningful. It is commonplace,
in this author's experience, for students to skip entirely any
tables they encounter in research reports. Although considerable statistical background is necessary for thorough analysis
of some tables, much can be learned from tables if the reader
can make three determinations: (a) what inference technique was
used? (b) how was the relationship studied? (e.g., comparing
averages, crossbreak, correlation coefficient); (c) what was the
probability that resulted? To answer these questions, you can
ignore much information in the tables.

TABLE 5.8
COMMON TECHNIQUES FOR TESTING STATISTICAL SIGNIFICANCE

Conditions	Technique
Testing difference between two arithmetic means when each group is larger than 30	Critical ratio
Testing difference between two arithmetic means regardless of group size	't' test for means
Testing differences among two or more arithmetic means	Analysis of variance and/or analysis of covariance
Testing differences between two groups when rankings rather than scores are used	Median test and/or Mann Whitney U Test
Testing statistical significance of a correlation coefficient	't' test for r
Testing significance of a relationship described in a crossbreak table	Chi-square (χ^2)

As you read research reports you may encounter a variety of ways of reporting statistical significance. One way is by attaching superscripts to significance values to be clarified in a footnote. This is illustrated in table 5.10. Another way of indicating significance is by using the symbol p for probability and the symbol < for less than. Thus the statement that the probability is less than .05 may be written symbolically as $p < .05$. The following examples may be helpful:

$p < .05$ means the chances of the relationship being due to chance are less than 5 in 100.

$p < .01$ means the chances of the relationship being due to chance are less than 1 in 100.

What does $p < .001$ mean? _____ [9]

_____

_____

[9]See page 204 for answer.

In this section several typical tables are presented for you to practice interpreting. The purpose is to show that you can learn much from tables with even the limited exposure to statistics provided by this book.

Table 5.9 shows several correlation coefficients. Each is the correlation between the two variables that it intersects (e.g., -.71 is the correlation between PSI-Control Scores and PSI-Communication Scores). These are scores on the test you examined in chapter two (pages 74-77). The purpose of the study was to see if these two test scores were related to ratings of teachers on several attributes. Notice that some correlations are positive and some are negative.

TABLE 5.9
CORRELATIONS AMONG PSI SCORES AND RATINGS
FOR A GROUP OF THIRTY-FOUR TEACHERS[10]

	PSI-Control	PSI-Communi-cation	Rigid Attitude of Right and Wrong	Acceptance of Self and Others
PSI-Communication	-.71**			
Rigid attitude of right and wrong	.57**	-.60**		
Acceptance of self and others	-.62**	.71**	-.75**	
Feelings of comfort and self-worth	-.44**	.52**	-.38**	.72**

**Significant at .01 level of significance.

Interpretation of Table 5.9: How were the relationships studied? _____

_____

_____

_____

_____

[10]Modified slightly from Rowan, N. T., "The Relationship of Teacher Interaction in Classroom Situations to Teacher Personality Variables," Table 9. (Unpublished doctoral dissertation, University of Utah, 1967).

Were some relationships statistically significant? _____

_____

_____

_____

If so, what do they mean? _____

_____

_____

_____

AUTHOR'S COMMENTS

Table 5.9 shows the correlations among five variables (two test scores and three ratings) for a group of thirty-four teachers. All the correlations are unlikely to be due to chance (significant at .01 level). They show that a high rating on acceptance of self and others is accompanied by a high rating on feelings of self-worth (r = .72) and low ratings on rigid attitude of right and wrong (r = -.38). They show also that high scores on PSI-Control are accompanied by low scores on PSI-Communication (r = -.71). Finally, and most important, they show that both the PSI scores are related to all ratings such that the teachers scoring high in control (and low in communication) are rated as lower in self-acceptance (r = -.62) and feelings of self-worth (r = -.44) and are rated as higher in rigid attitude of right and wrong (r = .57).

These results suggest that some teachers' behaviors are predictable from the tests used. An important point in interpreting any correlation is that it does not determine causation. For example, the correlation of .71 between rating of self-acceptance and tested openness of communication may mean that self-acceptance causes openness or that openness causes self-acceptance or that both are caused by something else (such as a secure childhood). Remember not to attribute causality to statements of relationship.

Table 5.10 pertains to the study described in chapter three (pages 93-96). The study investigated relationships between teacher behavior in the classroom and personality characteristics measured by tests. In this analysis a questionnaire type test called the Teacher Preference Schedule was used to separate the teachers into two groups—high in control need and low in control need. These groups were then compared on observer ratings of each teacher as to how kindly, stimulating, and controlling she was. The results are shown in table 5.10.

Table 5.10 is interpreted as follows: The title states that high and low need groups were compared on their mean ratings. We note that a 't' test was used. (Table 5.8 verifies that this procedure is appropriate for testing the significance of differences in means.) The asterisks following two of the 't' values indicate that the difference between means was significant on the ratings of kindly and controlling. The numerical values of the means show that the high need group was rated lower on kindly and higher on controlling. The difference for stimulating was not statistically significant. Notice that this interpretation can be made without knowing how the numerical values of 't' were obtained or what the numbers themselves mean.

TABLE 5.10

MEAN RATINGS OF TEACHER CLASSROOM BEHAVIOR AND 't' TESTS
FOR HIGH AND LOW NEED GROUPS
ON THE TEACHER PREFERENCE SCHEDULE[11]

Observer Rating	Low Control Need Group	High Control Need Group	't'
Kindly	10.94	7.88	3.73**
Stimulating	8.76	7.82	1.00
Controlling	7.53	10.59	3.87**

**Significant at .01 level of significance.

TABLE 5.11

ANALYSIS OF COVARIANCE RESULTS COMPARING CURRICULUM AND
COMPARISON GROUPS ON INTERPRETATION OF DATA TEST[12]

Source	S.S.	d.f.	M.S.	F	p
Between groups	47.5	1	47.5	4.5	<.05
Between classes within groups	831.7	18	46.2	4.4	<.01
Covariable	1319.2	1	1319.2	126.4	<.001
Error (within classes)	5010.3	480	10.4		

Table 5.11 presents results from the curriculum evaluation
study described in chapter four (pages 142-145). The purpose
was to compare sixth-grade students taught a particular social
studies curriculum with students not taught the program. The
groups were compared on several tests including the Application
of Generalizations Test, which you analyzed in chapter two
(pages 67-69) and Interpretation of Data Test used to illustrate
frequency polygons on pages 169-172. In interpreting this
table, try to determine how it relates to the purpose of the

[11]Modified slightly from Table 6.01 in Travers, R. M. W., Wallen,
N. E., Reid, I. E., and Wodtke, K. H., "Measured Needs of
Teachers and Their Behavior in the Classroom," Final Report,
U.S.O.E. #444 (8029)(1961).

[12]Taken from Table 7.2 in Wallen, N. E., Durkin, M., Fraenkel,
J., McNaughton, A., and Sawin, E., "The TABA Curriculum Devel-
opment Project in Social Studies," U.S.O.E. #6-10-182, (Menlo
Park, Calif.: Addison-Wesley, 1969).

study.   Note that one part of the table deals with a between groups comparison.

Interpretation of table 5.11:   How was the relationship studied (use table 5.8)? _____

_____

Was the relationship statistically significant? _____

_____

What additional information do you need in order to inter-pret the results (the additional information is presented on pages 169 and 172)?

_____

AUTHOR'S COMMENTS

Table 5.11. This formidable looking table contains a good deal of information that is of interest to a statistician, but which is not essential for interpretation. The table indicates use of analysis of covariance, which is used to test differences between group means or averages (see table 5.8). The value of p < .05 opposite the between groups entry under source indicates that the group means were significantly different at the 5 percent level. The remaining comparisons could be clarified by reading the description of the study, but are not of primary interest. Thus, all the remainder of the table can be ignored while deducing that a significant difference in group averages was obtained. Additional information is needed to tell which of the two group means was higher. The data on pages 169–172 show that the curriculum group scored higher.

Table 5.12 applies to the fictitious data used earlier in this chapter to illustrate crossbreak tables (page 175).

TABLE 5.12
COMPARISON OF THERAPEUTIC METHOD AND TRAINING INSTITUTION

| Institution | Therapeutic Method | | | |
	Rogerian	Gestalt	Behavior Modification	Freudian
Happy Valley State	7	20	10	8
Multiversity II	8	6	25	11
College of the Specific	15	10	5	5

Note: $\chi^2 = 27.81$, $p < .001$

Interpretation of table 5.12: How was the relationship studied? _____

_____

Was the relationship statistically significant? _____

_____

What does it mean? _____

_____

AUTHOR'S COMMENTS

The relationship was studied by means of a crossbreak table. The significant probability resulting from the Chi-square shows that the chances of the relationship being due to chance are less than 1 in 100. The institutions differ as to the therapeutic orientation of their graduates. It is not necessary to understand what the value of $\chi^2 = 27.81$ means nor how it was obtained in order to make these interpretations.

Limitations. Use of statistical inference procedures requires certain assumptions that are often difficult to meet in practice. They are frequently ignored in the reporting of research. Use of each of the procedures listed in table 5.8 requires certain assumptions regarding the data itself. For present purposes, we are ignoring these detailed assumptions. They have to do with such things as the shape of the distribution of the measurement in the population and the extent to which the measurements differ within groups. While these assumptions were necessary to the mathematician in developing the technique, some of them have been shown to be of relatively little importance because, even if they are not met, the statistical reasoning still holds. However, it is extremely important for our purposes to recognize that all of these techniques assume random sampling. As we have seen, the use of random samples in educational research is extremely difficult. As a result, the powerful techniques of statistical inference are frequently suspect when applied to educational research. If random sampling was not employed, the mathematician is likely to say that the techniques should not be used. In practice you will find that most studies report statistical significance whether a random sample was used or not. Whenever this is done, you should check to determine if the sampling procedures were random. If they were not, a serious question should immediately be raised about the assignment of statistical significance levels. It is sometimes argued that what is done in using significance levels without random sampling is simply establishing the probability that the results would be repeated in a hypothetical population from which the sample may be considered to be random. This is a very dubious procedure since one cannot define the population.

If the sampling is not random, the calculation of significance levels must be regarded not as a precise statement of probability, but simply as a rough guide to the likelihood of the results being repeated. Used in this way, they are useful. If a relationship is not statistically significant, we may feel justified in concluding that there is little basis for general-

izing the relationship. On the other hand, if an investigator
reports a probability of less than .01 for a particular relationship and his sampling procedure is not random, we must
recognize that the probability of this being simply a chance
finding *may be* considerably greater than the .01 that he has
reported.

What inference technique(s) is (are) appropriate for your

proposed study? _____

_____

_____

_____

Assuming you could carry out the computations, how confi-

dent would you be in reporting the results and why? _____

_____

_____

_____

SUMMARY

This chapter has acquainted you with some widely applicable
techniques for summarizing data and making it interpretable.
You have practiced applying them to a variety of examples and
have, hopefully, seen how they could be useful in your own
study. You have been introduced to the somewhat forbidding
topic of statistical inference and, presumably, have eliminated
some of the mystery from it. You will probably find that parts
of this chapter have more meaning for you as you begin to analyze the data from your pilot study.

Major concepts considered in this chapter:

Scatterplot	Quantitative variable
Correlation coefficient	Qualitative variable
Frequency polygon	Probability
Arithmetic mean	Statistical significance
Median	Inference techniques
Crossbreak	

REFERENCES FOR FURTHER READING

Edwards, A. L. *Statistical Methods*. 2d ed. New York, N.Y.:
  Holt, Rinehart & Winston, 1967.
Elzey, F. F. *A Programmed Introduction to Statistics*. 2d ed.
  Belmont, Calif.: Wadsworth, 1971.
Englehart, M. D. *Methods of Educational Research*. Chicago:
  Rand McNally, 1972. Chaps. 8, 9, 11, 13.
Helmstadter, G. C. *Research Concepts in Human Behavior*. New
  York, N.Y.: Appleton-Century-Crofts, 1970. Chap. 6.
Kerlinger, F. M. *Foundations of Educational Research*. New
  York, N.Y.: Holt, Rinehart & Winston, 1964. Chaps. 8–14,
  34, 35.
Tolbert, E. L. *Research for Teachers and Counselors*. Minneapo-
  lis: Burgess, 1967. Chaps. 2, 4, 5, 8.
VanDalen, D. B. *Understanding Educational Research*. 2d ed.
  New York, N.Y.: McGraw-Hill, 1966. Chaps. 13, 14.
Walker, H. M. and Lev, J. *Elementary Statistical Methods*.
  3rd ed. New York, N.Y.: Holt, Rinehart & Winston, 1969.

ANSWERS

Page 166: correlation coefficient for page 112 is .90; for
page 162, .23.

Page 174: median for curriculum group is 13.1; for comparison group, 11.8.

Page 192: The chances of the relationship being due to
chance are less than 1 in 1000 (.001 = 1/1000).

Critiquing Research Reports
or "How to Separate the Wheat from the Chaff"

INTRODUCTION

On completing this chapter you should be able to read and critique most educational research reports. You should also be able to write a results and interpretation section of a report and will have done so in relation to your pilot study. You will, in essence, have completed a research proposal.

You have now participated to some extent in all of the major aspects of designing and carrying out a research study. These include posing a question that can be feasibly investigated, clarifying terminology, justifying the importance of the study, stating hypotheses, developing adequate instrumentation, obtaining a good sample, recognizing limitations of generalizing from the sample, developing detailed procedures for carrying out the study, recognizing and attempting to control sources of bias (including extraneous variables and procedural bias), and using appropriate statistical procedures to clarify data. One aspect of this process, reviewing literature, has been treated only briefly in chapter one. You should now have the tools necessary to critically examine reported research and hence be able to do a more meaningful review.

CRITERIA FOR EVALUATING RESEARCH REPORTS

In reviewing a research study, one uses the same concepts that are important in designing a study. When designing and carrying out a study, one must focus on the various topics listed above and attempt to deal with them in the best way possible. In critiquing a study, one looks at the way in which the researcher dealt with these same problems. Table 6.1 presents an outline that may be useful in reviewing studies. You will notice that most of the material contained on the outline

pertains to topics that have been dealt with at some length
earlier in this book. There are, however, a few points that
need to be made at this time.

    Prior Research. Whenever one actually conducts a research
study, as distinguished from the learning process followed in
this book, it is presumed that he has taken the time to acquaint
himself with other studies that are pertinent to his question or
topic. That is, he examines prior research. Sometimes the research hypothesis is such that the area of related literature is
not very extensive. An example is the open classroom study. Although there has been considerable writing about the open classroom, very little research has been done concerning effects on
students. In other instances, it is difficult to know where to
draw the line, since there is a vast quantity of literature that
is somehow related to the research topic. For example, a large
amount of research has been done on the relationship between
amount of sensory stimulation in early childhood and subsequent
intellectual development. Not only is there a rather extensive
literature bearing directly on this topic, but there is a great
deal of literature generally related to each of the major variables, much of which could be considered pertinent. Ultimately,
it becomes a matter of judgment on the part of the investigator
as to how widely he will review literature. In reporting a
research study, it is expected that the author will include a
review of those studies that in his judgment are most pertinent
and important in relation to the study.

    In reviewing a particular study, it is often difficult for
the reader to judge whether the review of literature is sufficiently comprehensive and whether it includes the most pertinent
sources, since this requires a degree of expertise in the topic
being studied. There are, however, things that one can examine.
Whatever research or literature is cited, it should be clearly
related to the present study and the author should give at least
a brief summary of the results that the previous investigators
obtained.

    In reading a report, it is not uncommon to find a number of
studies mentioned, but with so little information provided that
the reader cannot assess either the relevance to the present
study or the importance of whatever findings emerged. Unfortunately, in reports published in most of the current journals,
the necessity of space saving often requires that the investigator drastically cut his literature review. Consequently, a
paucity of literature reviewed cannot totally be attributed to
the investigator. Nevertheless, the reader should still examine this part of the report according to the criteria mentioned
above.

TABLE 6.1
CRITERIA FOR EVALUATING RESEARCH REPORTS

Purpose—justification: Is it sufficient? Logical? Convincing?

Definitions: Are major terms clearly defined?

Prior Research: Is it extensive? Relevant? Are results summarized?

Hypotheses: Are they stated? Implied? Directional? Clear? Precise?

Sampling: Is the population clearly described? Implied? Is the sample clearly described? Is it representative? Random? Adequate size? Are limitations on generalizability presented?

Instrumentation: Is it adequately described? Is it reliable? Is it valid for the purpose?

Procedures: Are they clearly described? Are extraneous variables controlled? Is procedural bias controlled?

Data analysis: Are the statistics appropriate? Are limitations pointed out?

Results: Are they clearly presented? Is the written description consistent with the data? Are there a minimum of inferences?

Interpretation—discussion: Is it consistent with results? Is it relevant to the purpose? Does it place the study in broader perspective?

Results and Interpretation. The *results* of a study are the findings that have emerged in written form, usually with accompanying tables and/or charts. In examining a study, it is important to note whether the written description of the findings is appropriate and consistent with the data that are presented. In most cases, one will find this to be the case. Occasionally, however, there may be a discrepancy between the findings as reported in tables and the way in which they are described in writing.

The *interpretation* section of a report, in contrast, is where the investigator attempts to place his findings in a broader context. It is also the place for an investigator to recapitulate any difficulties that he encountered in the study and make suggestions for possible improvement in future studies.

It is of particular importance that the results and interpretation aspects of a study be kept distinct from each other ·
because a good interpretation section will typically go considerably beyond the data in attempting to place the findings in a
broader perspective. It is important that the reader not be
misled into thinking that the investigator has obtained evidence
for something that is only speculation. To put it somewhat differently, there should be no room for disagreement regarding the
statements in the results section of the report. The statements
should follow very clearly and directly from the data that were
obtained. However, there may be much argumentation and disagreement about the interpretation of these results.

Let us consider the results of the study relating teacher
personality and classroom behavior (page 78). As hypothesized
in that study, significant correlations of .40 to .50 were found
between a test of control need on the part of the teacher and
(a) the extent of controlling behavior in the classroom as observed, and (b) ratings by administrators as "less comfortable
with self" and "having more rigid attitudes of right and wrong."
These were the results of the study and should be clearly identified as such. In the interpretation section, however, one
might place these findings in a variety of controversial per-
spectives. Thus, one investigator might propose that this study
provides support for selection of prospective teachers, arguing
that anyone scoring high in control need should be excluded from
a training program on the grounds that this characteristic and
the classroom behavior it appears to predict are undesirable in
teachers. In contrast, another investigator might interpret the
results to support the desirability of attracting people with
higher control need into teaching. He might cite such data as
those reported in another example (page 78) to support the position that, at least in inner-city classrooms, teachers scoring
higher in control need are likely to have more businesslike
classrooms.

Clearly, both of these interpretations go far beyond the
results of the particular study. There is no reason why the
investigator should not make such an interpretation, provided
that it is clearly identified as such and that the impression is
not given that the results of the study provide direct evidence
in support of the interpretation. Many times a reported study
will sharply differentiate results and interpretation by placing
them in different sections of the report and labeling them accordingly. At other times, the two are intermixed, making it
difficult for the reader to sort out which are the results of
the study and which are the interpretations.

In the space below, report on your pilot study. If the
space provided is insufficient, use additional pages but report
on each category. This gives you a chance to practice writing

results and interpretation as well as to apply statistical procedures.

Sampling (On whom did you collect data?): _____

_____

_____

_____

Instrumentation (What instruments did you use?): _____

_____

_____

Procedures (How did you go about collecting data?): _____

_____

_____

_____

Data analysis (What statistics were used to clarify data?):

_____

_____

Results (What did you find out in relation to your hypothesis?): _____

_____

_____

Interpretation (What is the broader significance of your

results, assuming they were reproduced in your real study?): ___

_____

_____

_____

_____

Other (What did you learn about conducting research?): ____

_____

_____

_____

_____

CRITIQUING RESEARCH REPORTS

Your next task is to read and critique the following article that was published by the author and several colleagues a
few years ago.[1] Critique the study using the outline presented
in table 6.1. Discuss each of the topics outlined.

THE OUTCOMES OF CURRICULUM MODIFICATIONS DESIGNED TO FOSTER CRITICAL THINKING*

Norman E. Wallen, Vernon F. Haubrich,** and Ian E. Reid,
University of Utah

CRITICAL THINKING appears to be a universally accepted
objective of education though we are frequently unclear as
to what we mean by it and to what extent we wish to live
with its consequences. As has been pointed out elsewhere
(5) various definitions of critical thinking seem to encom-
pass some or all of the following features:

1. Use of scientific methods including emphasis on
evidence and the nature of hypotheses.

2. The tendency to be inquisitive, critical and ana-
lytical with respect to issues, personal behavior, etc. A
derivative of this attribute is lack of susceptibility to
propaganda.

3. Use of correct principles of logic.

---

[1]From the *Journal of Educational Research* 56 (July–August 1963).
Used by permission.

The emphasis is on the development of that elusive philosophical ideal, the rational man.

With respect to methods of fostering critical thinking two major approaches have been advocated. The first is "progressive education." Critical thinking is presumed to be but one of the objectives which are fostered by a greater degree of self determination, flexibility of curriculum and freedom of behavior. The results of the Eight Year Study provide some support for this position. Further support of an indirect type is provided by studies which indicate that questioning and critical behaviors are less likely to occur in rigid, highly formalized situations wherein deviation is punished (2).

The second approach emphasizes the tools rather than the attitude of critical thinking while recognizing the importance of a milieu conducive to the use of the tools. Thus emphasis is placed on acquainting students with the principles of logic and experimentation and with their use. It is this approach to which this study was directed.

METHOD

The basic design of the study was as follows:

It involved seven teachers of U.S. History (eleventh grade) in three Salt Lake City high schools who introduced the curriculum modifications and an additional two who served as controls. During the first year one class (selected at random) taught by each of the nine teachers was tested in the fall and again in the spring to establish the amount of gain to be expected over a year's time under the present curriculum. The tests used were the Cooperative U.S. History Test, the Watson-Glaser Test of Critical thinking and the I.D.S. Critical Thinking Test. During the summer of 1960, the experimental teachers attended a one week workshop on the University of Utah campus under the direction of Dr. Haubrich during which time they received training in the curriculum procedures and materials presently available as well as experience in the development of new materials. During the following academic year two of their classes were again tested in the fall and spring as were those of the control teachers. During this year, the staff members worked with the teachers in the utilization and development of materials. The resulting data permitted comparisons of gains made from year to year under the same teacher and from teacher to teacher within a given year.

The statistical analysis used was analysis of covariance, which permits comparison of end of year scores—

adjusted for beginning of year scores under the different
treatments. Thus (in effect) the mean gain achieved by the
experimental teachers during the first year—regular curriculum—is compared with the mean gain achieved under the
modified curriculum. Further, the mean gain achieved by the
experimental teachers using the modified curriculum is compared with the mean gain achieved by the control teachers
during the same year.

Curriculum Modifications

The overall plan of curriculum modification called for
the teaching of a unit in "critical thinking" followed
throughout the year by application to the content of the
course as rather broadly defined. As an example, the students were encouraged to examine their textbook, their
newspapers and their teachers for examples of fallacious
logic. This approach has been extensively developed in
the Illinois Curriculum Program under the direction of B.
Othanel Smith and his associates. In a comprehensive application of the plan in Illinois, a total of 36 teachers and
approximately 1,500 high school students in English, geome-
try, science and social studies classes participated. As of
this writing, only a preliminary report has been published
(5). It appears that the study was carefully conducted and
that the students experiencing the experimental method
showed greater gain on measures of critical thinking than
the control group without showing impairment in mastery of
course content.

Thus, the present study is, to a large extent, a replication of the Illinois study to determine whether similar
results are obtained—a procedure woefully lacking in educational research. In addition the present study contains
some methological improvements, notably the use of a "base
line" for gauging change which is based on the same teachers
who institute the curriculum changes.

For convenience, the curricular practices may be
divided into (1) materials presented during the unit on
critical thinking, and (2) materials used throughout the
remainder of the year.

1. *Unit on critical thinking.* This unit required approximately three weeks for all teachers and was conducted
—at the teachers convenience—sometime during the second or
third month of school.

The sequence of presentation varied from teacher to
teacher but included the following topics and in this general order:

a. Definitions—abstract and concrete
b. Logical fallacies—*post hoc* fallacy, etc.
c. Deductive principles
    Syllogisms
    If—then statements
    Validity and truth
d. Inductive principles
    The nature of evidence
    Analysis of arguments including recognition of
      implicit assumptions
    Reliability of sources

In addition to their notes and experiences during the workshop, the teachers were provided with copies of "Applied Logic" by Little, Wilson, and Moore and copies of "Guide to Clear Thinking" developed by the Illinois Curriculum Program. Also, it was intended that each student be provided with or have access to "A Guide to Logical Thinking" by Shanner. In one school, however, a misunderstanding resulted in these booklets not being available to all students.

As can be seen from the topics listed above, the intent was to present to these students many of the more salient developments in the areas of logic, semantics and philosophy of science but in a fashion which they would comprehend.

2. *Application.* Throughout the remainder of the year the teacher attempted to utilize the ideas and skills taught during the unit whenever feasible. To this end many of the exercises developed by the Illinois group were used. Also, the teachers showed considerable ingenuity and expenditure of effort in materials which they developed. Some of the flavor of the materials may be conveyed by the following illustrative exercises.

a. A statement on page 77 of the text states: "The Articles of Confederation granted considerable power to a Congress of the United States." Is this definition, explanation or opinion? What criteria are provided?

b. Analyze the argument for unfair advantages of big business on page 368 of the text. Are there irrelevancies? Fallacies? Do the reasons justify the conclusion?

c. Is there a fallacy in the following argument? Life under a strong central government in Great Britain was tyrannical. We must not allow a strong central government to develop in this country.

Tests Used to Evaluate Outcomes

The measuring devices used to assess the outcomes of the program included the Watson-Glaser Critical Thinking

Appraisal, the I.D.S. Critical Thinking Test, both con-
structed to assess skills in critical thinking, and the Cooperative American History Test, which was used to assess
change in the more typical content of the course.

   1. *Watson-Glaser*. This test was originally published
in 1942 and was revised in 1956. It contains five sub-tests:
inference, assumptions, deductions, interpretation and arguments. It has been used in numerous studies and is quite
adequate in terms of technical considerations such as reliability, norms, etc. Ennis (3) has, however, questioned its
validity on the grounds that some items are questionable and
that it gives too high a score to the "chronic doubter."

   2. *I.D.S. Test*. This test was developed in 1957 by
Ennis in part as an attempt to overcome his objections to
the Watson-Glaser. As such the items are on logical
grounds, superior. Preliminary data suggest that it is adequate from a technical standpoint.

   3. *Cooperative American History Test*. This test is
considered to be one of the best standardized tests of the
typical content of American History courses. It contains
items designed to test knowledge of historical facts; understanding of cause and effect relationships, trends and developments; and ability to recognize chronological relationships, interpret historical maps and locate historical information with emphasis on political and diplomatic history.
It is somewhat weak in the area of contemporary affairs.

Results

   Results of the analysis of covariance comparing students of the experimental teachers for the two years are
shown in Table 1. Table 2 shows the analysis of covariance
comparing experimental and control classes for the second
year only. Table 3 shows the means of the various groups as
well as some additional data pertaining to the I.D.S. Test.
Tables 4 and 5 show mean values for the Watson-Glaser and
Cooperative U.S. History Test respectively. These data
support the following interpretation:

1. *I.D.S. Test*

   a) Considered as a group, students of the experimental
teachers showed significantly greater gain ($p < .01$) the
second year, i.e. under the modified curriculum, as compared
to the previous year. The amount of the difference, when
compared to available norms, indicates the improvement to be
of practical importance. The students under the revised curriculum began the year with a mean score very near that
typical of eleventh graders and, by the end of the year

TABLE 1

ANALYSIS OF COVARIANCE—EXPERIMENTAL TEACHERS ONLY*

I.D.S. Test

Source of Variance	Σx^2	Σxy	Σy^2	d.f.	Adj. Σy^2	M.S.	F	P
Between years (curricula)	4	27	189	1	159	159	8.83	<.01
Between Teachers	423	347	428	6	168	28	1.56	
Interaction	187	229	489	6	287	48	2.67	<.05
Residual	8865	5066	10245	406	7350	18		
Total	9479	5669	11351	419				

Watson-Glaser

	Σx^2	Σxy	Σy^2	d.f.	Adj. Σy^2	M.S.	F	P
Between years (curricula)	44	58	77	1	15	15	.32	
Between Teachers	888	732	654	5	59	12	.26	
Interaction	1219	1374	1732	5	373	75	1.59	
Residual	28042	20298	31108	348	16414	47		
Total	30193	22463	33570	359				

Cooperative U.S. History Test

	Σx^2	Σxy	Σy^2	d.f.	Adj. Σy^2	M.S.	F	P
Between years (curricula)	904	-104	12	1	899	899	18.65	<.001
Between Teachers	1530	1235	1200	6	216	36	.75	
Interaction	634	725	1083	6	291	48	1.00	
Residual	23988	21601	39027	406	19575	48		
Total	27056	23457	41322	419				

*With the exception of the F column, decimals have been omitted to simplify the tables.

Cases were deleted at random so as to obtain samples of 20 each for each teacher for year 1 and 40 for each teacher for year 2. This procedure necessitated dropping the classes of one teacher from the Watson-Glaser analysis since only 12 students took both test and re-test during year 1.

TABLE 2
ANALYSIS OF COVARIANCE—EXPERIMENTAL VS.
CONTROL TEACHERS—YEAR 2 ONLY

I.D.S. Test

Source of Variance	Σx^2	Σxy	Σy^2	d.f.	Adj. Σy^2	M.S.	F	P
Between								
Groups	124	216	375	1	154	154	7.22	<.01
Residual	8203	5066	11352	386	8222	21		
Total	8327	5282	11727	387				

Watson-Glaser

Between								
Groups	254	206	167	1	24	24	.47	--
Residual	12262	13789	35229	391	19790	51		
Total	12516	13965	35396	392	19814			

Cooperative U.S. History Test

Between								
Groups	226	314	435	1	49	49	1.09	
Residual	22198	20397	36224	386	17481	45		
Total	22424	20711	36659	387	17530			

TABLE 3
MEANS OF EXPERIMENTAL AND CONTROL GROUPS IN THE PRESENT
STUDY AND OF OTHER COMPARISON GROUPS ON THE I.D.S. TEST

	N	Mean Fall	Mean Spring	Gain
Experimental Teachers – Regular Curriculum – Year 1	140	8.8	10.2	1.4
Experimental Teachers – Modified Curriculum – Year 2	280	9.1	11.8	2.7
Control Teachers – Regular Curriculum – Year 1	36	6.8	8.4	1.6
Control Teachers – Regular Curriculum – Year 2	53	7.5	9.0	1.5
Normative Data – High School Juniors*			9.0	
Normative Data – High School Seniors*			9.6	
College Educational Psychology Students*			12.3	
High School Students in Courses Emphasizing Critical Thinking*			12.1	

*Ennis, R. H. "Interim Report: The Development of the I.D.S. Critical Thinking Test."

TABLE 4
MEANS OF EXPERIMENTAL AND CONTROL GROUPS
ON THE WATSON-GLASER TEST

	N	Mean Fall	Mean Spring	Gain
Experimental Teachers – Regular Curriculum – Year 1	120	62.3	64.9	2.6
Experimental Teachers – Modified Curriculum – Year 2	240	61.6	64.0	2.4
Control Teachers – Regular Curriculum – Year 1	30	56.8	60.0	3.2
Control Teachers – Regular Curriculum – Year 2	53	59.6	62.0	2.4

TABLE 5
MEANS OF EXPERIMENTAL AND CONTROL GROUPS ON THE COOPERATIVE
U.S. HISTORY TEST (STANDARD SCORES: $\bar{X} = 50$, S = 10)

	N	Mean Fall	Mean Spring	Gain
Experimental Teachers – Regular Curriculum – Year 1	140	44.1	49.3	5.2
Experimental Teachers – Modified Curriculum – Year 2	280	41.3	49.7	8.4
Control Teachers – Regular Curriculum – Year 1	36	44.1	47.6	3.5
Control Teachers – Regular Curriculum – Year 2	51	39.5	46.9	7.4

scored at a level almost up to that of a sample of unse-
lected college students and almost as high as previously reported groups in high school classes emphasizing critical
thinking. Students of these teachers but without the revised curriculum showed the amount of gain to be expected
during the course of a year. Both groups began the year
with nearly identical mean scores.

   b) The significant ($p < .05$) teacher by method interaction suggests that the curricular modifications are more
effective with some teachers than with others.

   c) When students experiencing the revised curriculum
were compared with students in the regular curriculum
(during the same year—different teachers), they showed
significantly greater gain ($p < .01$). The gain for the students in the regular curriculum (two teachers) was almost
identical for the two years.

It seems legitimate to conclude that the revised curriculum had a rather marked effect on critical thinking as
measured by the I.D.S. Test.

2.   *Watson-Glaser Test.*

a)   The results for this test do not support the I.D.S.
Test results. There is essentially no difference between
the two groups of students taught by the experimental teachers in amount of gain. In both years, the gain is 2.8. The
group experiencing the modified curriculum was slightly lower on the fall testing. For the first year group, the gain
is from a percentile score of 77 to 83 while for the second
year group (modified curriculum) the gain is from the 74th
to the 81st percentile rank based on high school norms.
Grade equivalent scores are not available for this test.

b)   The comparison of experimental and control groups
during the second year only is consistent with the foregoing
analysis in showing no significant difference between the
groups.

The results for this test provide no evidence for the
modified curriculum. This finding is particularly disap-
pointing in light of the fact that the Illinois study did
find a significant superiority in amount of gain shown on
this test by the students in the experimental group.

3.   *Cooperative U.S. History Test.*

a)   Students under the modified curriculum made significantly more gain during the year than did students with the
same teachers during the preceding year (p < .001). In both
instances, the students at the end of the year scored slightly below national norms. The experimental group, however,
scored considerably lower at the beginning of the year.

b)   The experimental group (modified curriculum) showed
more gain than the control group during the same year, but
not significantly so.

c)   The control teachers achieved significantly
(p < .05) more gain the second year.

d)   The gain of the experimental teachers was not
significantly greater than the gain achieved by the control
teachers during the second year. Because of the gain
achieved by the experimental teachers we are tempted to
suggest that the curricular modifications may have fostered
greater interest and/or skill in dealing with the course
content, hence, greater mastery. But since the gain was not
significantly greater than that achieved by the control
teachers during the second year, it is possible that other
factors were operative, possibly that the second year students began the year with somewhat poorer background. It is
clear that the modifications did not result in a decrease in
the mastery of course content.

Reactions of teachers, students and parents. An additional measure of the outcomes of a plan such as this is to be found in the reactions of persons involved in it. Although no systematic attempt was made to collect such data in the present study, some information almost inevitably is present. It is recognized that impressions such as those which follow are subject to many criticisms on the grounds of selective sampling and bias of several kinds; they are nevertheless presented as valuable, though for the most part subjective, data.

1. The seven experimental teachers have all expressed considerable enthusiasm for the program as an interesting and worthwhile attempt in an important area, though some are quite skeptical as to the results achieved, particularly among the less able students. Even accounting for the expected desire to comfort the researchers and to justify their own efforts, it is our opinion that this represents an honest reaction on the part of the teachers. One bit of supportive data is that they have all indicated an intention to use at least part of the materials next year and have expressed the hope that further work of this kind will be undertaken.

The consensus seems to be that the material on fallacies and definitions was easiest to put across with the material on syllogisms the most difficult as would be expected. As to organization of presentation some of the teachers indicated that they would do it again in essentially the same way. Others would prefer to spread the topics out during the year and introduce them as smaller units and one teacher would, in the future, not teach the material as a distinct unit but rather would attempt to incorporate it throughout the course.

2. As reported by the teachers the reaction of students was varied. Some expressed the view that it was difficult. Others wondered what it was for, i.e. "Why don't we just have history?" Our expectation was that some students would be psychologically threatened by the material; this seems to have been the case but to a lesser extent than we expected. On the other hand some became intrigued and enjoyed it. Several teachers reported students making use of the material in arguments and particularly in debate, though some of the same material frequently is presented in debate (and in psychology courses). Several incidents of carryover to other activities were reported:

a) Letters were written to several advertisers and to a weather man requesting definition of terms. The former were not satisfactorily answered; the latter was — and in some detail.

b) As a result of a difference of opinion in class regarding a syllogism, several students wrote to a professor of philosophy at the University of Utah for clarification.

3. There appears to have been little reaction from parents. As expected, some parents feared that knowledge of history was being sacrificed for some new silliness, but the teachers were able to provide an explanation which was at least in some cases considered adequate.

We had expected some objection from parents along the lines that their children were beginning to question some of the eternal verities. That this did not happen may be attributable to parents confidence in the schools, to parental indifference or to lack of impact of our program.

Summary

This report describes a two year project which introduced into three high schools a curriculum plan designed to foster critical thinking and which attempted to assess its effectiveness. The curriculum plan was patterned after a similar program developed at the University of Illinois and consisted of the presentation of a three week unit on the tools of logical analysis, semantics and scientific method at a level appropriate to eleventh graders followed by application of these tools to the content of the course in U.S. History throughout the year. The seven participating teachers were provided a workshop prior to the introduction of the unit and were provided the services of the project staff, as well as the benefits of several group discussions during the year. Their interest and effort expended in the project was such as to leave no question but that the approach received an adequate trial.

The results of the evaluation demonstrate quite clearly that mastery of the typical content of the U.S. History course was not impaired by the curriculum modification. The effectiveness of the program in fostering critical thinking is not unequivocally demonstrated, since one of the tests to assess this change did not show any difference between experimental and control groups. The other test, however, which on logical grounds may be argued to be a better test, did show rather impressive differences in favor of students who received the revised curriculum. Further, the reactions of teachers and students, though not intensively studied, strongly support the value of the program.

Footnotes

*   This research received financial support from the Utah
    Educational Research Council.
** V. F. Haubrich is now at Hunter College in the Bronx.

References

1. Aschner, Mary J. "Teaching the Anatomy of Criticism,"
        The School Review LXIV (1956) pp. 317-22.
2. Carpenter, Finley. "Educational Significance of Studies
        on the Relation Between Rigidity and Problem Solving,"
        Science Education XL (1956), pp. 296-311.
3. Ennis, Robert H. "An Appraisal of the Watson-Glaser
        Critical Thinking Appraisal," *Journal of Educational
        Research*, LII (1958), pp. 155-58.
4. Ennis, Robert H. "Interim Report: The Development of
        the I.D.S. Critical Thinking Test," Personal Communi-
        cation.
5. Henderson, Kenneth B. "The Teaching of Critical Think-
        ing," *Phi Delta Kappan*, XXXIX (1958), pp. 280-82.

Critique

Purpose: _____

_____

_____

_____

Definitions: _____

_____

_____

_____

Prior research: _____

_____

_____

_____

Hypothesis: _____

_____

_____

_____

Sampling: _____

_____

_____

_____

Instrumentation: _____

_____

_____

_____

_____

Procedures: _____

_____

_____

_____

_____

_____

Data analysis: _____

_____

_____

_____

_____

_____

Results: _____

_____

_____

_____

_____

Interpretation: _____

_____

_____

_____

_____

Summary of critique: _____

_____

_____

_____

_____

AUTHOR'S COMMENTS

I view this article as an example of good research. It is
to be expected that I am somewhat less critical than others,
perhaps you.

Purpose—Justification: *The justification for the study,
presented in the introductory materials, relies principally
upon the premise that critical thinking is a widely accepted
objective of education and the implication that methods for
its development warrant further study. Further justification
is presented on page 212 where it is stated that the study is
a replication, with certain improvements, of a promising study
conducted in Illinois.*

Definitions: *The essential terms seem to be defined.*
Critical thinking *is defined in the introductory material. The*
curriculum modifications *are described in considerable detail,
and it is made clear that the outcomes are assessed operation-
ally through the use of three tests.*

Prior research: *The reference to prior research is not very
extensive. The two research studies cited, however, do appear
to be directly related to the study and the results of the
studies are indicated.*

Hypothesis: *The hypothesis of the study is not clearly
stated and it should be. It is, however, clearly implied that
those students receiving the curriculum modifications will perform in a superior fashion to those not receiving them.*

Sampling: *The sample was clearly not obtained in a random
fashion, involving as it did, seven teachers and three high
schools in one particular city. Neither the sample of teachers
nor students is adequately described. It would improve the
study if more information on both of these samples were included.
This limitation is partially offset by the fact that the study
is a replication of a study done elsewhere; and, assuming comparable results were obtained, the possibilities for generalizing would be greatly enhanced. However, it would still be important to have more descriptive data on the type of students
and teachers involved in both studies. An additional sampling
limitation is the small teacher sample size of seven. Also, the
authors fail to state the population to which they intend or
recommend generalizing.*

Instrumentation: *The instrumentation used is described in
some detail. The authors provide some assessment of reliability
and validity, although detailed information is not included. A
brief attempt at examining each test from the standpoint of
logical validity is included.*

Procedures: *The description of the situational manipulation
that was the crucial aspect of the study (i.e., the curriculum
modification) is described extensively, although one must*

acknowledge that in such a study precisely what occurred is difficult to describe completely. The study would have been strengthened by some observational data on the teachers at various times to support the contention in the summary that curriculum modifications were carried out as intended. The design of the study appears to be a good one. It permits comparison of curriculum and control classes during the same year; it also permits comparison of curriculum and control classes during two successive years while holding the teacher variable constant.

With regard to controlling extraneous variables, there is the possibility that the students in the curriculum groups differed in important ways from those in comparison groups at the outset because they were not assigned at random. The analysis of covariance procedure makes it possible to match the groups effectively with regard to the test data that was at hand, but cannot insure comparability of the groups on other variables. The problem is somewhat solved by the comparison of random classes of the same teacher in two succeeding years. One would not expect that the classes of seven teachers would systematically favor the curriculum group in the second year, although this is a possibility.

Loss of subjects probably introduces no systematic bias. Subjects were lost in one of two ways: by being absent on the days on which tests were given (unlikely to result in a systematic difference between the curriculum and comparison groups) and by being deleted during the statistical analysis (done randomly and should not introduce systematic bias). There is the possibility that extraneous events may have been responsible for any observed differences in the curriculum and comparison groups. The design of the study, comparing groups both across years and within the same year, however, is one of the best ways of attempting to rule out the effects of any particular extraneous event, because it would probably not favor either group under both circumstances. The factor of maturation should not be a problem in this study because it is held constant for the various comparisons made.

Attitudes on the part of both teachers and students might have produced procedural bias. In the event that the curriculum groups do show greater gain, there is the possibility that it is attributable to a general Hawthorne Effect rather than to the specific curriculum. Student attitudes toward the two differing curriculums would be important to study, but would probably not introduce a systematic bias. For example, if students preferred the modified curriculum, this would be a desired outcome and would not introduce a misleading bias. Attitudes toward testing would not be expected to differ for the two groups with the possible exception that the curriculum group might be more skeptical of the tests themselves and hence respond somewhat differently.

Objectivity of data collection is a problem in a study such as this.   The research report would be considerably improved by a description of how this problem was handled.   Who conducted the testing of students and handled the organization of data? Because all of the test data is machine scorable and capable of computer analysis, it seems unlikely that bias would be introduced at that point; but, the report should contain more information on this issue.   The crucial question is whether the techniques for collecting and analyzing data (the test scores) permit the possibility of bias.   The effects of sequential measurement should be ruled out by the design, since they would be comparable for all groups.   Instrument decay seems unlikely in this study.

Data analysis: *Analysis of covariance is appropriate for a study in which means are to be compared.   However, since random sampling was not employed, the authors should include a statement that the obtained probabilities are only approximate.*

Results: *The description of results is consistent with the tables presented and is clearly written.   The description is largely free of interpretive comments with the exception of a comment under the Cooperative History Test, which states that it is possible that certain factors were operating in one situation.   However, the wording seems to make it clear that this is an inference.*

Interpretation: *Relatively little interpretation is provided.   At several points the authors compare the findings of their study to that of the original, replicated study.   One might question the inclusion of the material on reactions of teachers under the results section because some of the statements are not clearly supported by the data presented within the study itself.*

Summary: *The principal criticisms of the study appear to be of two kinds: (a) The authors could have included additional detail on several points—particularly regarding the description of the sample and the testing procedures—and provided a word of caution with regard to statistical probabilities; and (b) the nature of the sampling raises questions about generalizing.   The fact that some of the results were similar to those of the previous study lends confidence to generalizing, but the fact that some results were not the same is a negative feature.*

Your next assignment is to critique two research reports following the format of the preceding critique. Use at least one of the studies that you summarized in chapter one (pp. 24-25). This exercise will be more valuable if at least one of your critiques is of a fairly sophisticated study, so you may wish to locate a new one. Summarize and critique each of these studies in the space provided. Follow the outline presented in table 6.1.

Study 1: (Reference: authors, title, journal, volume,

pages, year): _____

_____

Summary of study 1: _____

_____

_____

_____

_____

_____

_____

_____

Critique of study 1:

Purpose: _____

_____

_____

_____

Definitions: _____

_____

_____

_____

Prior research: _____

_____

_____

_____

Hypothesis: _____

_____

_____

_____

Sampling: _____

_____

_____

_____

Instrumentation: _____

_____

_____

_____

Procedures: _____

_____

_____

_____

Data analysis: _____

_____

_____

_____

Results: _____

_____

_____

_____

Interpretation: _____

_____

_____

_____

Summary of critique: _____

_____

_____

_____

Study 2 (Reference): _____

_____

Summary of study 2: _____

_____

_____

_____

_____

_____

_____

Critique of study 2:

Purpose: _____

_____

_____

_____

Definitions: _____

_____

_____

_____

Prior research: _____

_____

_____

_____

Hypothesis: _____

_____

_____

_____

Sampling: _____

_____

_____

_____

Instrumentation: _____

_____

_____

_____

Procedures: _____

_____

_____

_____

Data analysis: _____

_____

_____

_____

Results: _____

_____

_____

_____

Interpretation: _____

_____

_____

_____

Summary of critique: _____

_____

_____

_____

PROPOSAL

I suggest that you now pull together the various aspects of
your proposed study into one document, a proposal. This should
be relatively easy because it will primarily mean compiling the
statements you have made in various sections of this book. As
you have progressed through the book, some of your initial
statements and plans have probably altered. It should not be
too difficult to incorporate your changes. If you do this, you
will have a final proposal that should include all the various
strands of your material and will provide you with a culminating
product at the termination of the book.

The following proposal,[2] prepared by a student at the conclusion of this course, is an example of a proposal that I consider a good one at this stage of sophistication. It may be
useful as a general model. The report on the pilot study is
also included.

THE EFFECTS OF INDIVIDUALIZED READING
UPON STUDENT MOTIVATION IN GRADE FOUR

Nadine DeLuca

Purpose

The general purpose of this research is to add to the
existing knowledge about reading methods. Many educators
have become dissatisfied with general reading programs in
which teacher-directed group instruction means boredom and
delay for quick students and embarrassment and lack of motivation for others. Although there has been a great deal of
writing in favor of an individualized reading approach which
is supposedly a highly-motivating method of teaching reading, sufficient data has not been presented to make the
argument for or against individualized reading programs de-
cisive. With the data supplied by this study (and future
ones), soon schools will be free to make the choice between
implementing an individualized reading program or retaining
a basal reading method.

Definitions

Motivation: Motivation is inciting and sustaining action in an organism. The motivation to learn could be
thought of as being derived from a combination of several
more basic needs such as the need to achieve, to explore, to
satisfy curiosity.
Individualization: Individualization is characteristic
of an individualized reading program. Individualized reading has as its basis the concepts of seeking, self-selection,
and pacing. An individualized reading program has the following characteristics:

---

[2]Used by permission.

1) Literature books for children predominate.
2) Each child makes personal choices with regard to his reading materials.
3) Each child reads at his own rate and sets his own pace of accomplishment.
4) Each child confers with the teacher about what he has read and the progress he has made.
5) Each child carries his reading into some form of summarizing activity.
6) Some kind of record is kept by the teacher and/or the student.
7) Children work in groups for an immediate learning purpose and leave group when the purpose is accomplished.
8) Word recognition and related skills are taught and vocabulary is accumulated in a natural way at the point of each child's need.

Prior Research

Abbott, J. L., "Fifteen Reasons Why Personalized Reading Instruction Doesn't Work." *Elementary English* (January, 1972), 44:33-36.

This article refutes many of the usual arguments against individualized reading instruction. It lists those customary arguments then proceeds to explain why the objections are not valid ones.
It explains how such a program can be implemented by an ordinary classroom teacher in order to show the fallacy in the complaint that individualizing is impractical. Another fallacy involves the argument that unless a traditional basal reading program is used, children do not gain all the necessary reading skills.

Barbe, Walter B., *Educator's Guide to Personalized Reading Instruction*. Englewood Cliffs, New Jersey: Prentice-Hall, Inc., 1961.

Mr. Barbe outlines a complete individualized reading program. He explains the necessity of keeping records of children's reading. The book includes samples of book-summarizing activities as well as many checklists to ensure proper and complete skill development for reading.

Hunt, Lyman C., Jr., "Effect of Self-selection, Interest, and Motivation upon Independent, Instructional and Frustrational Levels." *Reading Teacher* (November, 1970), 24:146-151.

     Dr. Hunt explains how self-selection, interest, and motivation (some of the basic principles behind individualized reading), when used in a reading program, result in greater reading achievement.

Miel, Alice, Ed., *Individualizing Reading Practices*. New York: Bureau of Publications, Teachers College, Columbia University, 1959.
Veatch, Jeanette, *Reading in the Elementary School*. New York: The Roland Press Co., 1966.
West, Roland, *Individualized Reading Instruction*. Port Washington, New York: Kennikat Press, 1964.

     The three books listed above all provide examples of various individualized reading programs actually being used by different teachers. (The definitions and items on the rating scale were derived from these three books.)

Hypothesis

The greater the degree of individualization in a reading program, the higher will be the students' motivation.

Population

An ideal population would be all fourth grades in the United States. Because of different teacher-qualification requirements, different laws, and different teaching programs, though, such a generalization may not be justifiable. One that might be justifiable, though, would be a population of all fourth-grade classrooms in the San Francisco-Bay Area.

Sampling

The study will be conducted in fourth-grade classrooms in the San Francisco-Bay Area, including inner-city, rural, and suburban schools. The sample will include at least one hundred classrooms. Ideally, the sampling will be done randomly by identifying all fourth-grade classrooms for the population described and using random numbers to select the sample classrooms. As this would require excessive amounts of time, this sampling might need to be modified by taking a sample of schools in the area, identifying all fourth-grade classrooms in these schools only, then taking a random sample from these classrooms.

Instrumentation

Instrumentation will include a rating scale to be used to rate the degree of individualization in the reading program in each classroom. A sample rating scale is included on page 236. Those items on the left indicate characteristics of classrooms with little individualization.

Reliability: The ratings of the two observers who are observing separately but at the same time in the same room will be compared to see how closely the ratings agree. The rating scale will be repeated for each classroom on at least three different days.

Validity: Certain items on the student questionnaire (to be discussed in the next section) will be compared with the ratings on the rating scale to determine if there is a correlation between the degree of individualization apparently observed and the degree indicated by students' responses. In the same manner, responses to questions asked of teachers and parents can be used to indicate whether the rating scale is a true measure of the degree of individualization.

Another means of instrumentation to be used is a student questionnaire. A sample questionnaire is included on page 237. The following questions have as their purpose to determine the degree of motivation by asking how many books read and how the child indicates that he feels about reading: questions numbers 1, 4, 5, 6, 7, 9, 10, 11, 12, and 13. Questions 2, 3, 4, and 8 have as their purpose to help determine the validity of the items on the rating scale. Questions 14 and 15 are included to determine the students' attitudes toward the questionnaire to help determine if their attitudes are possible sources of bias for the study. Questions 8 and 9 have an additional purpose which is to add knowledge about the novelty of the reading situation in which the child now finds himself. This may be used to determine if there is a relationship between the novelty of the situation and the degree of motivation.

1. Basal readers or programmed readers predominate in room.	1 2 3 4 5	There is an obvious center in the room containing at least five library books per child.
2. Teacher teaches class as a group.	1 2 3 4 5	Teacher works with individuals or small groups.
3. Children are all reading from the same book series.	1 2 3 4 5	Children are reading various materials at different levels.
4. Teacher initiates activities.	1 2 3 4 5	Student initiates activities.
5. No reading records are in evidence.	1 2 3 4 5	Children or teacher are observed to be making notes or keeping records of books read.
6. There is no evidence of book summarizing activities in the room.	1 2 3 4 5	There is evidence of book summarizing activities around room (e.g., student-made book jackets, paintings, drawings, models of scenes or characters from books, class list of books read, bulletin board displays about books read. . .).
7. Classroom is arranged with desks in rows and no provision for a special reading area.	1 2 3 4 5	Classroom is arranged with a reading area so that children have opportunities to find quiet places to read silently.
8. There is no conference area in the room for the teacher to work with children individually.	1 2 3 4 5	There is a conference area set apart from the rest of the class where the teacher works with children individually.
9. Children are doing the same activities at the same time.	1 2 3 4 5	Children are doing different activities from their classmates.
10. Teacher tells children what they are to read during class.	1 2 3 4 5	Children choose their own reading materials.
11. Children read aloud in turn to teacher as part of a group using the same reading textbook.	1 2 3 4 5	Children read silently at their desks or in a reading area or orally to the teacher on an individual basis.

Student Questionnaire

Age _____   Grade _____   Father's work _____

                           Mother's work _____

1. How many books have you read in the last month? _____

2. Do you choose the books you read by yourself? _____

    If not, who does choose them for you? _____

3. Do you keep a record of what books you have read? _____

    Does your teacher? _____

4. What different kinds of reading materials have you read

    this year? _____

5. Do you feel you are learning very much in reading this

    year? _____ Why or why not? _____

6. Complete these sentences:

    Books _____

    Reading _____

7. Do you enjoy reading time? _____

8. Have you ever been taught reading a different way? _____

    When? _____ How was it different? _____

    _____

9. Which way of learning to read do you like better? _____

    _____ Why? _____

10. If you couldn't come to reading class for some reason,

    would you be disappointed? _____   Why? _____

11. Is this classroom a happy place for you during reading time? _____

12. Do most of the children in your classroom enjoy reading?

    _____

13. How much of your spare time at home do you spend reading just for fun? _____

14. Did you like answering these questions or would you have preferred not to? _____

15. Were any of the questions confusing? _____

    If so, which ones? _____

    How were they confusing? _____

Student Questionnaire:
Reliability: An attempt will be made to control item reliability by asking the same question in different ways and comparing the answers.
Validity: Validity may be questionable to some degree since school children may be reluctant to report anything bad about their teachers or the school. Observers will be reminded to establish rapport with children as much as possible before administering questionnaires and to assure them that the purpose of the questions does not affect them or their school in any way.
A teacher questionnaire will also be administered. A sample questionnaire is included on page 239. Some of the questions are intended to indicate if the approach being used by the teacher is new to her and what her attitude is toward the method. These questions are numbers 1, 2, 3, and 4. Question 5 is supposed to indicate how available reading materials are so that this can be compared to the degree of student motivation. Questions 6 and 8 will provide validity checks for the rating scale. Question 7 will help in determining a relationship between socioeconomic levels and student motivation.
Reliability: Reliability should not be too great a problem with this instrument since most questions are of a factual nature.

Validity: There may be a question as to validity depending upon how the questions are asked (if they are used in a structured interview). The way they are asked may affect the answers. An attempt has been made to state the questions so that the teacher does not realize what the purposes of this study are and so prejudice her answers.

Teacher Questionnaire

1. How long have you been teaching? _____

2. How long have you taught using the reading approach you are now using? _____

3. What other approaches have you used? _____

    _____

4. If you could use any reading approach you liked, which would you use? _____

    Why? _____

5. In what manner do you obtain reading materials? _____

    _____

    Where did you get most of those you now use? _____

    _____

6. How often are the children grouped for reading? _____

    _____

7. From what neighborhood or area do most of the children in this class come? _____

    _____

8. How do you decide when and how word recognition skills and vocabulary are taught to each child? _____

    _____

If it were feasible, an excellent instrument would be a parent questionnaire. The purpose of it would be to determine how much the child reads at home, his general attitude toward reading, and any changes in his attitude the parent has noticed.

Procedures

Since the sample of one hundred classrooms is large and each classroom will need to be visited at least three times for thirty minutes to one hour during each visit on different weeks, quite a large team of observers--probably around twenty--will be needed. They will work in pairs observing independently. They will spend about one-half hour each visit on the rating scale. The visits should take place between Monday and Thursday, since activities and attitudes are often different on Fridays. The investigation will not begin until after school has been in session for at least six weeks so that all programs have had sufficient time to function smoothly.

Control of extraneous variables: Sources of extraneous variables might include that teachers using individualized reading might be the more skillful and innovative teachers. Also, in cases where the individualized reading program is a new one, teacher enthusiasm for the new program might carry over to students. In this case it might be the novelty of the approach and teacher enthusiasm rather than the program itself that is motivating. An attempt will be made to determine if there is a relationship between novelty and teacher enthusiasm and student motivation by correlating the results of the teacher questionnaire (showing newness of program and teacher preference of program), indications from questions on student questionnaire, and statistics on motivation in a scatterplot. The influence of student socioeconomic levels on motivation will be determined by comparing the answers to the question on the teacher questionnaire concerning what area or neighborhood children live in, the question on parental occupations on the student questionnaire, and student motivation. The amount and availability of materials may influence motivation also. This influence will be determined by the answers of teachers concerning where and how they get materials.

Procedural bias: The presence of observers in the classroom may cause distraction and influence the degree of motivation. By having observers repeat procedures three or more times, later observations may prove to be nearly without this procedure bias. By keeping observers in the dark

about the purpose of the study, it is hopeful that will control as much bias in their observations and question-asking
as possible.

Data Analysis

Observations on the rating scale and answers on the
questionnaires will be given number ratings according to the
degree of individualization and amount of motivation respectively. The average of the total ratings will then be averaged for the two observers on the rating scale, and the average of the total ratings will be averaged for the questionnaires in each classroom to be used on a scatterplot to show
the relationship between motivation and individualization
in each classroom. Results of the teacher questionnaire
will be compared similarly with motivation on the scatterplot. The correlation will be used to further indicate relationships. (Note: These data analyses will be used similarly to their use in the "Open Classroom" study.)

PILOT STUDY

Procedure

The pilot study was conducted in three primary grade
schools in San Francisco. The principals of each school
were contacted and were asked if one or two reading classes
could be observed by the investigator for an hour or less.
The principals chose the classrooms observed. About forty-
five minutes was spent in each of four third-grade classrooms. No fourth grades were available in these schools.
The instruments administered were the student questionnaire
and the rating scale.

Both the questionnaire and rating scale were coded by
school and by classroom so that the variables for each classroom might be compared. The ratings on the rating scale for
each classroom were added together then averaged. Answers
on items for the questionnaire were rated "1" for answers
indicating low motivation and "2" for answers indicating
high motivation. (Note: Some items had as their purpose to
test validity of rating scale or to provide data concerning
possible biases, so these items were not rated.) Determining whether answers indicated high or low motivation created no problem except on Item #1. It was decided that fewer
than eight books (two books per week) read in the past month

indicated low motivation, while more indicated high motivation. The ratings for these questions were then added and
averaged. Then these averaged numbers for all the questionnaires in each classroom were averaged. The results were as
follows:

Room	Individualization	Motivation
#1	1.4	1.3
#2	2.1	1.6
#3	3.0	1.8
#4	3.2	1.7

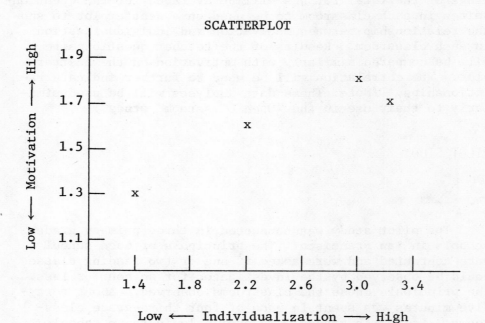

SCATTERPLOT

    Although this pilot study could not possibly be said to
uphold or disprove the hypothesis, we might venture to say
that if the actual study were to yield results similar to
those shown on the graph, there would be a strong correlation (estimate: r = .90) between individualization and motivation. This correlation is much too high to be attributed
to chance with a sample of 100 classrooms. If these were
the results of the study described in the research proposal,
the hypothesis would seem to be upheld.

Indications

Unfortunately, I was unable to conduct the pilot study in any fourth-grade classrooms which immediately throws doubt upon the validity of the results. In administering the student questionnaire, I discovered that many of the third-graders had difficulty understanding the questions. Therefore, the questioning took the form of individual structured interviews. Whether or not this difficulty would hold for fourth-graders, too, would need to be determined by conducting a more extensive pilot study in fourth-grade classrooms.

It was also discovered that Item #7 in the rating scale was difficult to rate. Perhaps it should be divided into two separate items--one concerning desk arrangement and one on the presence of a reading area--and worded more clearly.

Item #8 on the student questionnaire seemed to provide some problems for children. Third-graders, at least, didn't seem to understand the intent of the question. There is also some question as to whether the answers on Item #15 reflected the students' true feelings. Since it was administered orally, students were probably reluctant to answer negatively about the test to the administrator of the test. Again, a more extensive pilot study would be helpful in determining if these indications are typical.

Although the results of the pilot study are not very valid due to its size and the circumstances, its value lies in the knowledge gained concerning specific items in the instruments and problems that can be anticipated for observers or participants in similar studies.

SUMMARY

You have been involved in the process of designing and at least partially carrying out an educational research study. There is much more to be said in relation to each of the topics to which you have been introduced. Hopefully you will either now or at some later time delve more deeply into them. In any case, you are now in a position to read the majority of research articles in education with increased understanding and with appreciation for the difficulties and challenges involved in such research. This book, and in particular your written responses, should provide a useable way to review these materials when the occasion arises.

As important as the specific knowledge and skills, however, is the attitude, which I hope has been fostered by this book, that educational research provides a means for obtaining knowledge vital to the improvements in education that are so desperately needed, and that it can be an exciting and interesting challenge as well.

REFERENCES FOR FURTHER READING

Borg, W. F. *Educational Research*. 2d ed. New York, N.Y.: David McKay, 1971. Chap. 17.

Travers, R. M. W. *An Introduction to Educational Research*. 2d ed. New York, N.Y.: Holt, Rinehart & Winston, 1964. Chap. 15.

VanDalen, D. B. *Understanding Educational Research*. 2d ed. New York, N.Y.: McGraw-Hill, 1966. Chaps. 15, 16.

The following are compilations of research reports with accompanying analyses and guides to critical review.

Cook, D. R. *A Guide to Educational Research*. Boston: Allyn and Bacon, 1965.

Lehmann, I. J., and Mehrens, W. A., eds. *Educational Research— Readings in Focus*. New York, N.Y.: Holt, Rinehart & Winston, 1971.

Glossary-Index

Ability Test, 59–72

Analysis of Variance, 192

Application of Generalizations Test, 66–71

Applied research, 2

Arithmetic mean, 174

Average, 174

Basic research, 1

Bias, *influences that affect a study in unintended ways and distort the findings*, 126; see Sources of bias of researcher, 28

Chi-Square, 192

Clarification (of research question), 7–16

Contamination, *influences that prevent an adequate test of the research hypothesis*, 117; see *also* Bias

Contingency Table, 175

Correlation coefficient, *a numerical index of the degree of relationship between variables*, 165, 166

  Pearson Product Moment, 168

  Spearman Rank Order, 168–70

  and prediction, 166–67

Critical ratio, 192

Critiquing a study, 205, 210, 224–26

Crossbreak, 174–78

Data, *the basic information collected in a study, usually expressed numerically*, 158–204

Definition, dictionary, 7

  operational, *clarification of a term by specifying the operations (actions) taken to identify or measure it*, 7

Design, 111

  Single group, 111–12, 116, 158

  Multiple group, 111, 113

Experimentation, 120

Extraneous variable, *a variable outside the direct control of the researcher that affects a study in unintended ways*, 117–23; see *also* Sources of bias

Frequency polygon, 171

Feasibility, 3

Generalizing, 86, 90, 92, 95–100, 102–108

Hypothesis, *a predicted outcome of a study*, 26

  advantages of, 27–28

  as relationship, 29–30

  directional, 32–34

  limitations of, 27–28

  nondirectional, 32–34

Indicator, 37–42

Interpretation (of results), 207

Instrument, *the device used to collect data*, 44

Interview, 42–44

  structured, 53–59

Justification, 22–26

Mann Whitney U Test, 192

Matching, 122

Measurements, *the index (score) derived from an instrument*, 45

Median, 174

Observation record, 48–52

Open Classroom Study, 3

  examples from, 3, 6–10, 17, 23–24, 27, 29, 36–45, 48–52, 71–72, 79–80, 84–86, 88–92, 112–16, 117–24, 158–64, 187

Picture Situation Inventory, 72–78

Pilot Study, 156

  example of, 241

Population, *the group to which results are generalized*, 87

Prediction

  and correlations, 166–67

  and hypothesis, 26

Probability, 186

Procedural bias, *a distortion introduced into a study through the procedures used*, 123–24; see *also* Sources of bias

Procedures, *arrangements made for data collection and methods of analyzing relationships*, 111

Projective test, 72–78

Proposal, 231

  example of, 232

Questionnaire, 58–59

Ratings, 36–42

Reference materials, 18–20

Related studies, 17–22, 206

Reliability, *consistency of measurement*, 45–48, 61–64, 78, 82

Replication, *repetition of a study*, 88

Results, 207
Sample, *the individuals on whom data are collected*, 84
  cluster, 87
  description of, 88-90
  random, *a sample drawn so that each individual in the defined population has an equal chance of being included*, 87, 88
  representativeness of, 87
  size, 84-85
Scatterplot, *diagram for portraying a relationship between two variables*, 112, 159, 160, 162
Sources of bias
  attitude of subjects, 127, 136, 140, 147, 151
  effects of sequential measurement, 128, 137, 142, 147, 152
  extraneous events, 127, 136, 140, 146, 151
  instrument decay, 129, 137, 142, 147, 152
  location selection, 127, 136, 140, 146, 150
  loss of subjects, 127, 136, 140, 146, 150
  maturation, 127, 136, 140, 147, 151

objectivity of data collection, 128, 137, 141, 147, 152
  subject selection, 126, 136, 140, 146, 150
.Statistical inference, 186-203
  Techniques, Table of, 192
  limitations of, 202
Statistical significance, *the probability that the results of a study are due to chance*, 190
Stating the problem, 2, 6
't' test, 192
Validity, *whether an instrument measures what it is intended to measure*, 45-52, 56-58, 64-66, 69-71, 76-78, 81-82
  logical, 45, 49-50, 52, 56-58, 64-66, 69, 76-77, 81
  empirical, 45-49, 52, 58, 70-71, 78, 82
Variable, *any characteristic that can take different degrees of quantity or quality*
  quantitative, 174
  qualitative, 174
Watson-Glaser Critical Thinking Appraisal, 66, 211

Student Questionnaire

Please evaluate each of the following by rating and commenting.

	Excellent	Good	Fair	Poor
1. Use of one study (open classroom) for examples throughout the book.	☐	☐	☐	☐

Comment: _____

_____

| 2. Use of author's research for examples. | ☐ | ☐ | ☐ | ☐ |

Comment: _____

_____

| 3. Use of assignments involving other resources (e.g., observing, interviewing). | ☐ | ☐ | ☐ | ☐ |

Comment: _____

_____

| 4. Requesting written responses periodically. | ☐ | ☐ | ☐ | ☐ |

Comment: _____

_____

| 5. Use of author's comments following written responses. | ☐ | ☐ | ☐ | ☐ |

Comment: _____

_____

	Excellent	Good	Fair	Poor
6. Relating content to development of student's own proposal.	☐	☐	☐	☐

Comment: _____

_____

| 7. Writing style. | ☐ | ☐ | ☐ | ☐ |

Comment: _____

_____

| 8. Selection of content (concepts, factual information). | ☐ | ☐ | ☐ | ☐ |

Comment: _____

_____

| 9. Adequacy of content coverage. | ☐ | ☐ | ☐ | ☐ |

Comment: _____

_____

| 10. Difficulty level in general. | ☐ | ☐ | ☐ | ☐ |

Comment: _____

_____

| 11. Difficulty level of chapter 5. | ☐ | ☐ | ☐ | ☐ |

Comment: _____

_____

_____